Brahmrishi Yoga
200 Teacher Training

Margot Milcetich

Lisa Thiel, Editing and Layout

Brahmrishi Yoga Publications

Publisher: Brahmrishi Yoga Publications
BrahmrishiYoga.org

Date: December 2014

Printed in United States of America

ISBN: 978-1503372085

MANTRAS

Mantra before Teaching

Om saha naavavatu
Saha nau bhunaktu
Sahaviryam karavaavahai
Tejasvi naavadheetamastu
Maa vidveeshaavahai

As we move in to this time of sharing
May we be protected by the Oneness
May our joy and energy increase
May our learning shine on our faces
May we be free from (jealousy) thoughts
and emotions that divide us

Gayatri Mantra

Om bhur bhuvah svahah
Tat savitur varaanyam
Bhargo devasya dhimahih
Dhiyo yo nah prachodayat

Oh! earth, space, and galaxies
The splendor that is realized
May that light illuminate our intellects
May we always be near to That

Closing Mantra

Asato maa sad gamaya
Tamaso maa jyotir gamaya
Mrityor maa amritum gamaya

May we be led from unreal to real
May we be led from darkness to light
May we be led from death to immortality

Om Shantih Shantih Shantih

Om, peace in the heavens
Peace in the space around us
Peace in every heart

Table of Contents

Appendix

PREFACE

The flow of the training is based on the teaching of Kapil who taught Samkhya in an early Vedic era. The Vedic era took place thousands of years BCE, and was an oral tradition long before the knowledge was written down. Veda means knowledge and these extensive texts describe how life can be lived well, offering principles of sacrifice, mantra, health and spiritual knowledge. Kapil took an unusual turn with his knowledge. He offered 22 short aphorisms that he called a "nutshell philosophy," outlining why detachment serves us better than trying to appease the gods through sacrifice. His basic tenet is that we cannot control the forces of nature outside of ourselves, but we can work to alleviate our personal suffering in the face of change.

The fundamental power is observation. We are the seers and the knowers of our lives. We are also what is seen and what is known. Our living system with all its powers of moving, grasping, perceiving, learning and discerning, is an energetic sea of fluctuation. The discrete outline of all our instruments is the first item of importance in Samkhya and the most daunting. Why learn all the pieces and parts? The answer is clear: so that we may not mistake our real self for any partial experience. Our real self, the anchor of our being lies with our power of observation. What keeps us from our own wholeness is a partial vision. What brings us to wholeness is clarity of thought, discipline and discernment, that is, an intellect that can guide us.

This hatha yoga manual rests on the bedrock of 22 inclusive Samkhya aphorisms. Each of the twelve chapters rests on the perspective of one or several of these statements. The aphorisms are short; each one opens a span of meaning offering a discrete view of the yogic path. Each view gives direction and support for the yoga method.

We believe that everyone who comes to a hatha yoga session is a whole person. Each whole person is connected to the oneness of the source of life and is an integrated expression of that source. But the sustaining experience of oneness is dim. We seek to find what we have lost—the fullness of what we are and the capacity to hold that experience. The chapters of this manual give us the knowledge for creating an integrated practice. Our goal is to become facile teachers.

Action is said to be the means for the sage who seeks to climb the heights of Yoga; but when he has climbed the heights of Yoga, tranquility is said to be the means.
Bhagavad Gita 6/3

Chapter One – Tranquility

SS 1 How to Remove Pain
The 22 Samkhya Sutras and Practice

The story of the first chapter: The purpose of yoga is to remove suffering. This is the opening of the Samkhya Sutras and the beginning of our inquiry into yoga. Read all 22 Samkhya verses, and institute a home practice that includes movement and stillness. Our subtler instruments of knowing are best observed in silence. A home practice is the laboratory of our inquiry into yoga and how to become a teacher. Without witnessing the value of the yoga methods within our own bodies and minds, we will have little to impart to others. We begin in hatha with moving gently, understanding principles of movement and range of motion. Have compassion for the tissues of the body. Resistance is our friend, matching the moods and difficulties of our lives.

  ➢ What can we expect of the movement of our limbs?
  ➢ How can this body art help us find an unlimited source of energy and awareness?

Contents

Forms are limiting boundaries; for there to be one form,
others must be excluded. What is to be known is without limits.
Huston Smith

PHILOSOPHY

Samkhya Sutra 1: Now, How to Remove Pain

The philosophies of Samkhya and Yoga, two of the six systems of ancient Vedic knowledge, address suffering. The other systems advise how to live and act, and include the fields of atomic theory, logic, health, ritual, and ultimate cause. Within limits, technology and social systems can alleviate the suffering of the human condition. But the solutions are not permanent. We are not always in control of solutions outside ourselves. What remains under our control is the mind. The suffering that is driven by our own minds is addressed by the practices of yoga and the underlying philosophy of Samkhya. Buddhist thought derives from the same basis. The principle concept is:

heya, heya hetu, hana, hana upaya.	
Heya	the avoidable, that is, suffering
Heya hetu	the avoidable can be ended
Hana	there is a method
Hana upaya	the method can be applied

A key inspirational verse in Patanjali's Yoga Sutras is based on this same philosophy: heyam dukham anagatam II/16. "The suffering that has not yet come is to be avoided." The implication is that the suffering of the past is over and the future holds any suffering we might encounter. We take care of the future by attending to what is happening "now." The future arrives in the present moment.

Attachment comes from a lack of understanding as to what makes us happy. Like a deer that roams the forest seeking the source of an enticing smell that is its own musk, in the same way, we mistakenly seek fulfillment outside ourselves. Once we have found what seems to make us happy, then we cling to those experiences, not realizing that experience has simply awakened the enjoyer. The enjoyer is the real self. An unchanging experience of the real self is ultimately what satisfies our yearning. The world around us will always change. If our anchor is external, we will be unsettled. If we find how to connect with ourselves, directly and profoundly, we can remain free from suffering.

Our external attachments are also called identifications: the ego accept the limits of partial experiences as the self. The mind experiences life through the senses and mind and the ego evaluates and organizes those experiences. Freedom lies in letting go or suspending those identifications in the service of finding a deeper self that is not dependent on circumstances. If we can see our external attachment as a problem and our freedom from attachment as a solution, then we can effectively practice.

As an ocean becoming filled by rivers remains unmoved,
he who is unmoved as the rivers of desire enter
attains peace; not so the desirer of desires.
Bhagavad Gita II/70

Brahmrishi Yoga

Brahmrishi Yoga is inspired by Brahrishi Vishvatma Bawraji, 1934-2002, who revived the ancient teaching of Samkhya philosophy as the basis of yoga. Our guru asked us to teach Samkhya philosophy. Its fundamental analysis was central to his interpretation of yoga, and its value has been lost over time.

According to the Indian system of philosophy, each of the six systems has a companion philosophy.[1] The teaching of Samkhya is traditionally paired with Yoga. The message Swami Bawra revived is that one absolute source projects into life as both the knower and the known, that is, as the light of consciousness and a field of energy. We find freedom in life by valuing both distinct powers. Our guru often called his teaching realistic idealism: "real" because the philosophy defines the values and accepts the limits of energy, and "ideal" because it highlights the values of consciousness.

Samkhya Philosophy and Teacher Training
The ancient Vedic teaching of Kapil's Sāmkhya philosophy underlies the arc of this teacher training manual. The order in which Kapil presents his knowledge creates an outline and a series of lenses through which we can comprehend yoga—a path to freedom from suffering.

Yoga
Patanjali, a more modern teacher than Kapil, from about 2500 years ago, compiled the Yoga Sutras, which describes the many practices of yoga. Our freedom from suffering lies in finding the real self as seer, an unwavering source of integrated well-being, a profound connection with a source of existence, intelligence, and a state of blissfulness.

Two main emphases of the practices of Yoga derive from Kapil's original distinction between thought and breath. Thought is related with consciousness and refinement of thinking. Breath is related with vitality and energy in service of knowledge,

---

[1] The six systems are Sāmkhya and Yoga, Vedanta and Karma Mimansa, Nyaya and Vaishika.

consciousness, and freedom, rather than in service of one's limited self. The two fundamental paths of thought and breath, or knowledge and devotion, are also found in the distinction between Samkhya and Yoga—one is analysis, the other, a heart-felt practice.

Samkhya Philosophy and the Theory of Causation

Swami Bawra emphasized that spirituality is a science. The aim of spiritual science is to realize the source of our life. Knowledge is necessary for an effective practice. Our practice is most fruitful when we have a clear understanding of our real position: our individual existence is not separate from the source of life.

Kapil relies on the theory of causation to explain the relationship between the source of life and individual existence. This theory holds that whatever exists in the cause will appear in the effect, and, likewise, whatever exists in form must be found in its cause. Cause and effect are two states of the same truth, not two different truths. An effect contains the properties and qualities of its source, as a clay pot is an individual form of clay but has the same properties and qualities of the clay from which it was made.

Following this logic, Kapil established that each human being is an effect of the supreme cause and has the properties and qualities of the supreme source, but in a different state or stage. Spiritual science teaches that we can realize the supreme cause in our current position, in the present moment. This realization of oneness with the source is not beyond our reach; it can be approached with logic, wisdom, understanding, effort, and practice.

Our sense of existence comes from awareness and intelligence—what we call consciousness. Consciousness is defined as truth, knowledge and infinity. In Vedic language, consciousness is considered the soul and the self. Our individual soul functions through five energetic levels: the sheaths of intellect, ego, mind, senses, and body. When consciousness is active at any one of these levels then it assumes the parameters of that sheath. Thus we have intelligence consciousness; ego consciousness, which is awareness of our I-amness; mind consciousness or thought; awareness associated with the activity of the senses; and physical awareness or identification with the body.

Instead of a sense of oneness and wholeness, we experience limitation in countless ways, from believing we are our bodies and our social identities to fearing death as the end of our existence. The practices of yoga aim for the realization that our own awareness or sense of existence is independent of this physical system and therefore is not bound by the limitations of the body or mind.

In Samkhya these sheaths are discussed as projections of energy or transformations of energy. The fact that consciousness is active within different forms of energy does not limit consciousness. To use fire as an example, fire appears as a flame giving light and heat. Fire is not limited to that one flame; it appears where fuel is present. The appearance or disappearance of a flame is related with the fuel, which is limited, but the element of fire exists regardless of fuel. The purpose of yoga practice and meditation is to understand consciousness as separate from the limitations of energy. As fire burns with fuel, our consciousness functions through the sheaths. Consciousness has its own properties and qualities unrelated to the limitations of the instruments through which it functions. Consciousness is infinite and eternal.

The manifestation of consciousness by virtue of the medium of energy is the essence of the teaching. The medium is energy. We have difficulty seeing energy as a medium of manifestation. We see it as who we are. Samkhya will teach us that we find our real self as a seer and a knower. For that we need to refine our instruments of knowing so the light of consciousness can shine.

Samkhya Sutras

Sutra 1: Now, how to remove pain—the nutshell principles. Suffering can be avoided by application of a method. This approach to the dilemma of our humanity is the basis for yoga practice.[2] Kapil begins by stating his purpose. In the remaining twenty-two aphorisms Kapil analyzes how to attain that freedom.

Sutra 2: Eight root causes. There are eight root causes: nature or prakriti, intellect, ego, sound, touch, form, taste and smell. This second sutra establishes the principal existence of nature or energy. Prakriti is the causal, unmanifest and formless state of nature. Intellect[3] is the first projection of nature, pure light, from which all the rest sprouts. It is causal energy. The other six are subtle energy.

Sutra 3: Sixteen modifications. The eight root causes of nature have sixteen modifications, forming the complete expression of all diversity. The vibrations of sound, touch, form, taste and smell transform into the elements of space, air, water, fire and earth. Ego moves as mind receiving information from the five cognitive senses of ears, skin/proprioception, eyes, tongue and nose. The mind acts through the body with the instruments of mouth/tongue, hands, legs, and the generative and eliminative organs. All sixteen are forms of gross energy. The eight root causes along with the sixteen modifications are twenty-four aspects of the objective world. Thirteen of these aspects are instruments of gaining knowledge and eleven are related to the transformation of energy into the gross matter of the physical universe.

---

[2] The philosophy of Buddhism has its roots in Sāmkhya and is based on the same principle of removal of suffering: *Heya, heya hetu; hana, hana upaya.*
[3] Intellect is called *mahatattva*, the great principle on the cosmic level and *buddhi*, the intellect on the individual level.

Sutra 4: Purushah. After the diversity of energy is explained, Kapil introduces the second eternal principal, spirit. Purusha means indweller. Purusha is consciousness; its qualities are truth, knowledge, and infinity, or existence, intelligence, and bliss. The real self, the essence that we seek, lies in consciousness. Identifying self with the forms of energy is the source of suffering.

Kapil first establishes that the two eternal principals of prakriti and purusha exist. This is the key to the philosophies of Samkhya and Yoga. Freedom from suffering comes with the realization of the distinct and separate qualities of nature and spirit. Both are eternal, but spirit is stable and nature is always changing and transforming.

Sutra 5: Three attributes. Nature changes due to an imbalance among its three attributes or gunas of light, movement and stability, also correlated with causal, subtle and gross energy. The name of nature, prakriti, includes three attributes: light (pra), movement (kri), and stability (ti). The two eternal principal of nature and spirit manifest due to disequilibrium in these three attributes. The imbalance comes with the inspiration of consciousness, which initiates plurality and multiplicity. Countless beings come into form, each one an expression of nature and spirit. Nature is transformative. Spirit remains one and unchanging.

Sutra 6: Evolution and involution. Because of the movement of the gunas, nature evolves from a formless state into form and then involutes back into a formless state. This occurs within smaller cycles and within the vast cycles of time. Individual beings go through a process of evolution. Through a long process, nature develops all the instruments whereby a human being has the capacity and responsibility to understand and realize the source of the two eternal principles. Through a process of evolution the instruments are developed through interactions with nature. In human life, the instruments have reached a fully developed state, whereby we can consciously serve life while reflecting the values of consciousness—truth, knowledge, and bliss. The full experience of consciousness is dependent on the development of the instruments.

Sutra 7: Suffering due to self, other beings and the divine world. Multiplicity within the movement of the three gunas is not a smooth experience. Our suffering can be understood in light of the three qualities. We suffer due to ourselves in three ways: illness of the body, weakness of the mind, and impurity of the intellect. Yoga practice addresses these through asana, pranayama, and meditation. Suffering due to the imposition of other beings and the devastations of natural disasters cannot be avoided, but the effects are tempered by the inner strength of detachment from nature.

Sutra 8: Five sources of knowledge. There are five sources of knowledge, the five buddhis: the intellect, ego, mind, the five cognitive senses, and the five active senses. The word for intellect is buddhi. According to Samkhya and Yoga, all instruments of nature are for learning and emancipation rather than enjoyment. Bhoga means enjoyment through experience. Yoga means liberation through experience. Ultimately, liberation comes with purity of the intellect, which guides our practice with discernment and reflects the pure light of consciousness. Instruments that have been developed through the evolutionary process of nature can now be refined through our yoga practice.

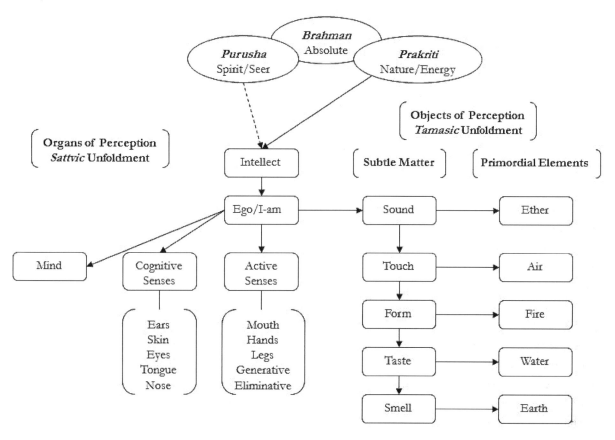

Sutra 9: The five causes of action. These are evidence, fallacy, fancy, sleep and memory. We act based on the content of our buddhi, our intellect. Evidence is often called right knowledge; it is accurate perception and comprehension. Fallacy is a wrong perception; it is our imagination or speculation. Sleep is a dull state of the intellect, and memory is a trace of previous experience that determines our action. Mostly we live in ignorance of truth and we are prompted by fallacy and fancy. Truth means we understand the real nature of the self as consciousness, not energy.

The instruments of gaining knowledge are activated by the twins of thought and breath, elaborated in sutras nine and ten. Five different states of our intellect shape our reality and therefore cause our action, and each state of the intellect is supported by breath or energy as the means to pursue the desired path of action.

Sutra 10: The five winds. These are movement of life energy in the body: upward movement, downward movement, heat generated at the center, energy that spreads outward to every limb, and an energy that feeds the senses in the head and brain. In the Yoga system these are collectively known as prana, although the first, the upward movement, is also called prana. The other four are apana, samana, vyana, and udana. These five main movements of energy support all vital functions of the body; with our vitality we bring thought into speech and action. (See Chapter 7 for diagram.)

Sutra 11: The five souls of action. Self-restraint, practice, dispassion, stable intellect, and wisdom give action focus and value for spiritual development. The first, self-restraint is yama, of which there are five: non-violence, truthfulness, non-deception, control of emotion, and non-accumulation. These five vows of self-restraint reduce our projection of energy into the environment and keep us in balance with others. With this containment, the other souls of action can be fruitful. Practice and dispassion work together: we detach from outward craving and seek inwardly for the real self. The fruit is a stable, non-fluctuating intellect that can guide us with wisdom. These five give us clarity, right knowledge, and the energy for freedom. Otherwise, if we get caught in wrong knowledge and fancy, infatuation will keep us tied in the five knots of ignorance.

The following five knots of ignorance elaborate the results of action based on one of the five shapes of the intellect, false knowledge. Each and every action we undertake will give its result in our karma, an unending source of bondage unless freedom is sought.

Sutra 12: The five knots of false knowledge. Darkness, infatuation, great infatuation, aversion, and blind aversion bind us to ignorance of the real self. The darkness of disconnection with the source covers the intellect. Then the ego becomes infatuated with itself, since it does not see its source in light and knowledge. Then attraction to outward objects and relationships take precedence over the real self. With attractions come aversion and fear of loss, and finally the great fear of death.

Sutra 13: Twenty-eight-fold inabilities. These keep us in ignorance. Thirteen are handicaps within the ten cognitive and active senses, the mind, ego and intellect.

Sutra 14: Nine-fold satisfactions. Of the twenty-eight-fold inabilities, five keep us from applying effort: contentment with the pleasure of the five senses, and complacency that nature, and the ideas that the right time, means and luck will take us forward.

Sutra 15: Eight gifts or perfections. The final eight inabilities are a lack of any of the eight gifts that assist us: wisdom, sound or mantra, study, divine grace and service, and an experience of freedom from the three kinds of suffering.

Sutra 16: Ten root objects or primary qualities. The ten root objects are the properties of nature and spirit as they manifest into form. Four belong to both: principal existence, union, disunion and finite existence. Three belong to nature: oneness, purpose, and existing for others. Three belong to spirit: separation from energy, plurality, and non-doer. Discerning the effects of nature and spirit manifesting into form is the analytic practice of Samkhya. This core analysis comes only after we understand that we are mostly lost in this matrix of energy and we need to discern finely and wisely in order to stay clear of the pitfalls of infatuation with the forms of energy.

Sutra 17: Emanation is accumulation. Without accumulation of energy into form, we would not see the effects of the projection of energy. The caution of the previous sutra is supported and kindly amplified with an additional understanding of nature. Nature will create and accumulate around us all that we need for experience and growth. The universe is not merely an accumulation of gross elements; every experience of childhood, livelihood, community and family is the means for us to learn from the results of our previous actions. We have in front of us at all times an accumulation of the perfect means for our growth. This is nature's great gift.

Sutra 18: Fourteen stages of evolution of beings. There are five lower forms of life: vegetable, insect, reptile, bird, and mammal. Human life stands alone as unique. As humans we have developed all instruments and, with the intellect, we have the capacity to realize our self as one with the source of life. We can find freedom from suffering. There are eight higher levels of divine life, but there is no means for learning and the development of the soul in the higher levels. Within a human body we have the capacity for gaining liberation.

Sutra 19: Three-fold bondage. We are bound with attachment and identification to each level of the projection expression of energy: gross, subtle, causal.

Sutra 20: Three-fold emancipation. Liberation comes with detachment from all projections of energy, described as "gradual, disembodied, and singleness."

Sutra 21: Three proofs. Seeing, inference, and testimony. The testimony of others gives us the knowledge we need to move ahead. From that testimony we can infer the truth. Our goal is to see with our own eyes.

Sutra 22: If a person comes to realize what I have told, he will be free from the effects of all actions and from bondage. He will never again be the prey of threefold suffering.

"…walk… don't run."
Swami Bawra 1985

We gradually cultivate and our practice becomes stable.
We cultivate stability and our practice grows gradually.
Devhuti

Knowledge is the ground of yoga. Practice is the art of yoga.

PERSONAL PRACTICE

The two steps of progress toward freedom from suffering are knowledge and practice. Yoga is a "spiritual science," with a body of knowledge called Samkhya, and a research method called Yoga.

Truth in the practice of yoga is what becomes stable in our experience and correlates with what becomes stable or consistent in the lives of others. It is shared experience along the lines of shared principles. The main experiment for you within yoga is the research you undertake within your own experience. It is subjective, not objective.

The value of truth is its indifference. Truth does not care about our moods or whether we accept or reject the truth. Truth applies universally to all situations and all people. William James[4] coined a phrase for the truth that underlies our seeking, "the perennial philosophy." The knowledge is constantly revived by our own need to know and to seek.

All treatises on Yoga are based in ancient texts called the Veda. Veda means simply "knowledge." The etymology of the word Veda is "to see." To know and to see within our own experience is the value of the knowledge. The practices of yoga come from an ancient tradition of first learning to know, then to cultivate ourselves within the light of that knowledge, and then to realize or see. It is a subjective process. We are seeking to be seers.

Definition of Yoga
The definition of yoga is in the second verse of Patanjali's Yoga Sutras. "Yoga is the stillness of the modifications of the intellect."

yogas chitta-vritti nirodhah		Yoga Sutras (YS) 1/2
yogas	Union with the source	
chitta	Causal energy, the intellect or buddhi in Samkhya	
vritti	Fluctuation, modification	
nirodhah	Ending, inhibition, stillness	

The opening of each spiritual discourse or treatise on philosophy begins with the highest knowledge first. If one can understand this verse, the teacher's work is finished. If the knowledge is not fully comprehended, the teaching continues.

---

[4] *The Varieties of Religious Experience*, William James, 1902

The Fundamentals of Practice and Detachment
Patanjali adds: "The ending of fluctuations or waves of cognition occurs by practice and non-attachment."

abhyasa-vairagyam tan-nirodhah		YS 1/12
abhyasa	Practice: Exertion toward stability, sthiti, toward a tranquil flow of cognition devoid of fluctuation, and vigilance in remaining there. Practice Requires uninterrupted continuity in time and of focus. YSI/14	
vairagyam	Non-attachment: Detachment from cognitive fluctuation, i.e. inhibition of disturbance.	
	A deeper level of vairagyam is freedom from desire. YS I/15	
tad	Of those: Refers to waves or fluctuations.	
nirodhah	Inhibition: Restriction, ending.	

The word for practice is abhyasa. It is paired with non-attachment, vairagyam. Non-attachment is another way of saying detachment. In other words, we let go of attachment for the purpose of practice. Attachment is identification of self with a partial experience. Detachment does not make us less humane; it simply makes us less attached to personal gain as the main motive for action. Practice means to seek the real self.

The Qualities Needed for Practice
Patanjali tells us: "In the case of others (practitioners), the detachment that emerges from practice is preceded by faith, energy, memory, cognitive absorption and primary insight."

shraddha-virya-smriti-samadhi-prajna-purvaka itarsam		YS 1/20
shraddha	Faith: provisional, flexible, non-dogmatic, but with respect for the practices.	
virya	Vigor: reverential faith gives energy, vigor.	
smriti	Memory: with memory, practice can proceed with continuity and intentness.	
samadhi	Absorption: with a one-pointed practice, absorption comes.	
prajna	Insight: this state comes in samadhi when the intellect is stable. Then, wisdom and right knowledge are the state of the intellect. Intuition is a natural phenomenon.	
purvaka	Preceded by, conditioned upon.	
itaresam	Of the others.	

Practice is an art. Teaching is an art. Application of science is an art. The culminating practice of meditation has aptly been named "the science of being and the art of living."[5] Through knowledge we cultivate ourselves in practice. To help our yoga students gain freedom from suffering, the heart of yoga practice, the application of method begins with us.

---

[5] Maharishi Mahesh Yogi.

Meditation and the Koshas

Kapila was the first teacher to develop a systematic approach to freedom from suffering. Our sense of existence, I-amness, comes from awareness of consciousness. Within a later teaching, the *Taittiriya Upanishad*, the layers of our energetic instruments were termed sheaths. The teaching establishes that our conscious essence, our I-amness is covered by five sheaths called *koshas*. The coverings are bliss, intelligence, the mind (including both perception and volition), vital energy, and matter. In Samkhya these sheaths are discussed as projections of energy or transformations of energy. The concept of sheaths simplifies the Samkhya model and helps us visualize how to move inward.

When our I-amness is active at any one of these levels it experiences the qualities related with the specific sheath. Thus we may experience bliss; intelligence; mind as an active power and a displayer of perception; our vital energy called *prana*; and awareness of the physical system. Yoga philosophy incorporates these sheaths into three bodies that constitute our human existence.

Causal Body: Anandamaya Kosha

The causal body of a human is an individual medium. This medium is the first projection of energy. It resides at the core of every being. Within this medium the qualities of pure consciousness are expressed or manifested. These qualities are existence, intelligence and blissfulness.

The medium has two primary characteristics. First, it manifests the qualities and properties of what is near it. An example of a crystal is used to explain this. If a red flower is next to a clear crystal, the crystal will appear to be red. The crystal is pure, but it adopts the color of the flower. Similarly, this medium adopts the qualities of consciousness, bringing into our lives a lively intelligence and a stable existence, which is experienced as bliss. The manifestation of pure consciousness in the medium is called the individual soul or I-amness; the experience of bliss is the first covering of our I-amness.

Secondly, the medium is similar to a computer chip; it holds our experienced knowledge. A very small chip made from a tiny piece of silicon is capable of holding a vast number of instructions. Our individual medium is even smaller than a computer chip, yet holds millions of impressions from our previous lives. These impressions structure our intelligence and are the cause of our belief system, abilities, actions, and current physical form. These impressions form the second covering called *vijnanamaya kosha* or the intelligence sheath and structure our subtle body. The subtle body includes three *koshas*: *vijnanamaya*, *manomaya*, and *pranamaya*.

Causal Body

anandamaya kosha
(bliss)

I-amness
Form-bliss

Subtle Body

vng
vijnanamaya kosha
(intellect)

manomaya kosha
(mind)

pranamaya kosha
(vital energy)
    subtle energies:
    sound, touch,
    sight, taste, smell

Intellect: think, decide
impressions, belief

Mind: displayer, volition
ego perception, senses

Vital energy: activates
senses, energizes body

Gross Body

annamaya kosha
(physical body)

Primordial elements:
    space
      air
        fire
          water
            earth

ananda

vijnana

manas

prana

anna

Meditation

The purpose of meditation is to understand consciousness as separate from the limitations of energy. Consciousness, in the form of I-amness, functions through the sheaths.

Once we have isolated our I-amness, we can analyze its properties and qualities to determine its true nature and its source. Initially, I-amness is experienced free from the limitations of the external world, but it retains an individual and limiting quality. Gradually, as meditation deepens, the source of I-amness is experienced directly and a state of oneness, unity, or wholeness is realized, free from any limitation or comparison.

In meditation, we work from the gross level toward the subtle—we seek inward in stages.

> ➢ If our body and senses are quiet because we have disengaged from outer stimulation, can we find a sense of existence independent of this activity?
> ➢ At the level of the mind, can our individual identity exist undefined by mental impressions? If so, what are the properties and qualities of I-amness? Is I-amness limited?
> ➢ Is there something beyond our individual existence and intelligence that encompasses us?
> ➢ Is there something beyond I-amness that has the capacity to observe or know?
> ➢ Do existence and awareness exist beyond the limits of our instruments or sheaths?

Guidelines for Meditation

Find a focal point within each layer of the koshas...

Body: Ground in the base of body.
Find the structure and weight of the heavy bones.

Breath: By observing breath, we quiet the senses and turn them inward.
Turn three senses inward on the breath: see, feel, and listen.
Find the vitality of the breath.
Observe the muscles of breathing.

Lengthen the breath: Count as a way to train the mind; count the length of the exhalation first. After a minute, increase the length of the inhalation to match it and add a count at the suspension before the exhalation and at the pause before the inhalation.

Mind: Quiet the perceptive mind; let go of content; return gently to the breath.

In meditation, we satisfy the mind's need for activity by focusing on a repeated sound, a *mantra*. A *mantra* is a vibration or sound related with the source of life. This sound helps the mind concentrate inwardly. The ability of the *mantra* to help the mind focus is enhanced by relating the sound with breath.

Find the I-am as observer, witness, thereby settling of the agency of the ego.

Intellect: Notice the role of the intellect to guide the process.
We are from infinity and we reside in infinity.

Metaphor: Encourages a deepening of the process. It adds content and meaning.

Ocean of energy and consciousness and waves of breath...
Inhale and *receive* vitality; exhale and *surrender*...
All beings are breathing from the same space; the same oxygen is supporting all life...

So-ham Meditation Instruction

The *So-ham* mantra is mentioned in an ancient text called the *Isa Upanishad*. *So-* indicates that supreme source. *-Ham*, pronounced *hung*, indicates our individual existence or I-amness. *So ham* means "Whatever I am seeing as the source—That I am."

1. Begin by observing the inflow and outflow of your breath through the nostrils.

2. Once settled into a gentle, rhythmic pattern, add the sound of *So-* to your inhalation and the sound of *-hung* to your exhalation.

3. Allow your breath to flow easily, silently repeating the mantra with each inflow and outflow of breath.

4. Whenever your attention drifts to thoughts, feelings, images, or sensations in your body, gently return without judgment, and continue the focus on the breath with the sound of the mantra.

5. Continue for 15 to 30 minutes.

6. Slowly transition to your daily activity.

Experiences during meditation may include: repeating the mantra; thoughts, feelings or images; sleep; or an experience of pure awareness. The mantra may change, become vague, or follow a rhythm. Just continue the process, effortlessly focusing on your breath and mantra, and allow the changes to come and go.

Whenever you notice that your focus has drifted away, gently bring back your attention without judgment to the process. If you fall asleep, then the body and mind needed rest. Once you awaken, resume meditation even for a few minutes if your time is completed.

If you notice there has been a time without thoughts or mantra yet you were aware, then this is an isolated experience of our individual existence connected with its source in consciousness. I-amness is one with that seer. Gradually this quiet witness will become a part of our everyday awareness.

Meditation is not for tuning out; it is for tuning in. It is not for getting away from it all; it is for getting in touch with it all. You will find that the value of meditation is not found specifically in meditation but in a more enjoyable and fulfilling life.

TECHNIQUE

Guidelines for Building a Home Movement Practice

---

breathe

same time	same place	empty stomach
awareness first	eyes closed	turn inward
energize standing	breath of joy	warrior
release lying down	knees to chest	rest

---

breathe

find flexibility in spine   lengthen spine
open side to side
forward fold
twist
open back

open joints	knees	ankles	wrists	neck	shoulders	hips

---

strength	balance
body awareness	counterpose
find a sequence that works	use it for a while
no hurry	no worry
less is more	
breathe	

---

turn inward more deeply in relaxation – then sit and linger in balance

Farhi's Moving Principles

Donna Farhi describes seven moving principles in her book, Yoga Mind Body & Spirit (Henry Holt and Co., 2000). These principles are ways of feeling the movement of the body and enhancing the integrity of movement. The seven are: breathe, yield, radiate, center, support, align and engage. Each is an awareness practice. While reading Donna's descriptions, we gain a feeling not only for the principle but for the importance of language. In the following anatomy section you will learn precise terms and concepts. The value of anatomy is to learn about healthy movement in the joints and limbs. The virtue of moving well and aligning the body in the poses is to cultivate balance and health in the body, clarity and focus in the mind, thereby freeing our awareness from the simple bondages of ill-health and confusion. Below are Farhi's seven moving principles as she defines them.

1.	Breathe	—Let the breath move you.
2.	Yield	—Yield to the earth: weight and gravity.
3.	Radiate	—Move from the inside out: the human starfish.
4.	Center	—Maintain the integrity of the spine: the central axis.
5.	Support	—Establish foundations of support: structural building blocks.
6.	Align	—Create clear lines of force: alignment and sequential flow.
7.	Engage	—Engage the whole body: the democratic body community.

Return the mind to original silence, developing clear perception.

ANATOMY

Range of Motion and Stretching

When we open a class, our intention is to draw the students into their experience. Beginning with the first warm-up, our intention is to focus the students inward. During warm-ups, we do not merely heat the body (the original use of the term), we create congruence between the body and consciousness by breathing and centering so that the mind is not wandering. Thus we can begin to attend to subtler internal experience. During warm-ups, we breathe, orient the mind, simultaneously open the joints, and play with the range of motion.

Safe stretching[6] is based on neuro-anatomical principles. We have an elegant system of restraint in the body that allows us to safely move. If we understand restraint we can enhance our range of motion. The limits of the body are what make the body and its functions elegant.

Terminology
The anatomical position of the body from which we orient movement is with the front of the body facing out, arms down at our sides, and palms facing forward.

Abduction	to draw away from the midline
Adduction	to draw toward the midline
Extension	to increase the joint angle
Flexion	to decrease the joint angle
Rotation	to turn around a given point
Anterior	toward the front
Posterior	toward the back
Superior	toward the head
Inferior	toward the feet
Medial	closer to the midline
Lateral	further from the midline
Frontal	divides body into front (ventral) and back (dorsal); also called the horizontal plane
Median	midline plane dividing body left or right; also called the sagittal plane
Transverse	divides body into upper and lower

---

[6] The following sections are derived from *Stretching without Pain*, by Paul Blakey (out of print), and *The Key Muscles of Hatha Yoga*, Volumes I & II, Ray Long M.D., 2006, 2008.

Three kinds of joints in the body
In order of most to least movement:

Synovial	Freely moveable; joints whose range of motion is important for movement and stretching
Cartilaginous	Slightly moveable, e.g between vertebrae and ribs/sternum
Fibrous	Relatively unmovable, e.g. sutures in the skull, and between the tibia/fibula (calf) and radius/ulna (forearm)

Structure of a Synovial Joint
The joint cavity is very small.

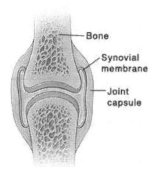

The joint capsule is a sleeve-like extension of the bone covering of the articulating bones. The capsule is a complete casing around the ends of both bones joining them together.

Articular cartilage covers and cushions the end surfaces of each bone.

Menisci are an extra layer of articular cartilage most commonly injured in knee trauma.

Synovial membrane is a slippery membrane that lines the inner surfaces of the joint capsule. It secretes synovial fluid that lubricates and feeds the interior of the joint. Synovial fluid is the most effective lubricant known to man; it is thin and has low viscosity.

Ligaments are cords of dense white fibrous tissue that bind the joint.

Normal Range of Motion
Normal range of motion should be enough to meet our needs. To extend beyond a normal range is to risk reducing the effective binding value of ligaments and cartilage. The value of effective stretching is to train the body to maintain a normal range of motion.

Neck is a Pivot Joint. First cervical vertebra (the atlas) has complete rotation on top of second cervical the axis). Avoid full circles. Stretch sides, up and down, rotation with head erect, all independently. Mild nose circles release unconscious gripping.

Shoulders have Ball and Socket Joints. Humerus to scapula is a shallow joint that allows for greater range of motion than the similar hip joint, but at the same time makes it more vulnerable to dislocation.

Elbows are Hinge Joints. A woman's elbow has a larger hollow in the distal end of the humerus, which allows many women to straighten beyond 180 degrees and appear "double jointed."

Wrists are Gliding Joints. Carpal bones together assist the range of movement. In the intercarpal area, each of the eight carpal bones has a small movement that adds up to a complete range of motion.

Thumbs are Saddle Joints. This gives them versatility.

Spine: degree of rotation varies with location e.g. cervical vs. lumbar.

Hips are Ball and Socket Joint. The placement of the femur into the acetabulum is much deeper than the shoulder joint, which means the joint has less range of motion than the shoulder, but more stability.

Knees are like Hinge Joints with some Lateral Movement. Knees favor flexion and extension and have the potential to sustain stress of lateral movement. Vigorous body rotation with the feet planted firmly on the ground can result in a tearing of the meniscal cartilage in the knee.

Ankles are Hinge Joints with lateral movement sustained by Gliding Joints.

Connective Tissue
Understanding connective tissue will help you visualize a safe stretch. Not all connective tissue is safe to stretch. Ligaments that support the structure of synovial joints will tear when stretched beyond 6 %. Tendons that connect muscles to bones are not supposed to be stretched. We want the joint capsule to remain stable. It is the fascia surrounding the muscle tissue that we stretch. There are two fascial layers: superficial fascia lies under the skin in the dermis and deep fascia sheaths surround muscles. The deep fascia tissue covers each muscle fiber, groups of individual muscles, and an outermost sheath of muscle that includes all smaller sheaths.

Connective tissue is comprised of elastic fiber and collagen, a fibrous protein that provides strength. Connective tissue surrounds individual muscle fibers, bundles of fibers, and larger groups of fibers. The tissue that surrounds muscles is contiguous with the ligaments and tendons, denser connective tissue, and the bones themselves.

Connective tissue shrinks with aging (and with sugar intake). Inflexibility accelerates aging. When connective tissue is used, it responds by replacing protein. Thus use creates health in the tissue.

Connective tissue that surrounds the muscles is more mobile when warm. It is crystalline and solid when cold and almost liquid when warm. The risk of injury is reduced when the tissue is warm.

Physical stress on the body decreases the aging process. Astronauts age quickly without the pressure of the atmosphere. Isometric exercise was invented by the Russians for space travel in the 1950's.

Ligaments can safely stretch and reshape after a few weeks of rest. However if repeatedly stretched, ligaments become slack and the joint is more likely to be injured. Ligaments are composed of white fibrous tissue. A ligament is pliant and flexible, which provides freedom of movement. Bones break more easily than fibrous tissue tears.

Yellow elastic tissue contains more lipids (hence its color) than white, and is found in places in the body where greater flexibility of the connective tissue is important, such as the fascial sheath in the lower back. White and elastic tissue are mostly parallel constructions.

Tendons join muscle to bone and are made of white fibrous tissue. They have few blood vessels and nerves (exception is the Achilles tendon). The connective tissue surrounding the muscles extends into the white fibrous tissue of the tendons. Elastic and non-elastic tissues seamlessly join, and stretching beyond 4% can result in irreversible deformity.

Fascia stretches. Fascia is full of spaces (areolae) that allow for fluids to move freely through the tissue. Fascia is a general binder and one of the most extensive types of tissue found in the body. It sheaths muscles and is found in viscera. The fibers are interwoven rather than parallel. Note: Fibromyalgia is a condition of binding fascial tissue.

Resistance to flexibility in order of most to least:

Joint capsule and ligaments	47 %	✗	Not safe to stretch
Muscle fascia	41 %	✓	Safe to stretch
Tendons	10 %	✗	Not safe to stretch
Skin	02 %	✓	Safe to stretch

Problems of Aging

Over time scar tissue and injuries restrict our range of motion. Bad postural habits combined with shrinking and tightening connective tissue lead to compression in the joints and contribute to the problem of reduced synovial fluid in the joints. Activities that counter the problems of aging, such as yoga, lead to an improved quality of life.

Muscles and the Nervous System

(Note: this is a brief introduction to muscles and the nervous system; the topic will be covered in more detail in Chapter 6.)

We stretch connective tissue by activating the musculoskeletal system. That activation is initiated by the nervous system, and the subsequent movement gives feedback to the nervous system through a sensory system embedded in the muscles and tendons.

Skeletal muscle is striped. Cardiac and smooth muscle (viscera) do not need to be stretched. From its normal resting length a striated muscle can contract 70% or stretch 130%. A striated muscle is arranged in parallel muscle fibers that converge towards the tendons. Fascia stretches with the muscles.

A muscle fiber is a soft, contractile substance enclosed in a tubular sheath. Coiling of proteins causes muscles to contract. The neuromuscular junction is where the nerve terminates in the muscle fiber. At the junction, an electrochemical signal stimulates the flow of calcium, which initiates the shortening of the muscle.

A muscle fiber contracts completely or not at all. The way we vary strength is by recruiting more motor units as the load increases (a motor unit = one nerve ending connecting to 100 muscle fibers). Crucial to neural control is a feedback system. The sensory nerves that give information related to movement are called proprioceptors.

Strength and Length

Shortened muscle memory: A used muscle (in contraction) that is not lengthened will reduce the range of motion. The muscle is more liable to retain lactic acid and other by-products of metabolism. Also an over-used muscle is subject to scarring and may shorten during healing, especially if not passively stretched. On the other hand, after stretching, strengthening exercises reestablish muscle tone.

The best muscle training includes dynamic strength training through the full range of motion.

Proprioception: Muscle, Tendon, Joint Sense

There are two kinds of stretch receptors, one measuring magnitude of contraction, the other the rate of contraction. Spindle cells are stretch receptors found in the belly of the muscles. They detect muscle length and send sensory messages into the spinal cord, which activates motor neurons. These motor neurons tell the muscles to contract if they go beyond a pre-determined length. Stretching deeply and quickly stimulates a powerful protective contraction. Successful stretching starts slowly and builds length gradually.

Magnitude of contraction is measured in the tendons by the Golgi tendon organs. When a muscle contracts, the tendon receptors detect the load on the muscle and have the capacity to release the action of the muscle when the tension on the tendon goes past a pre-determined level. This prevents injury. It occurs when the signals from the Golgi tendon organ are greater than those from the muscles.

Joint receptors signal the orientation of the body in space and the position of body parts. Other receptors sense pressure, vibration, pain, direction and speed of motion. This variety of sensory input influences reflex motor responses. A sensory protective reflex, such as adduction of the inner thighs that activate when our feet slide apart on ice, prevents movement beyond a safe range of motion.

Stretching
Contraction is an intelligent part of stretching and there are three basic types. Isotonic contraction is with movement and is most frequently used during exercise. Isometric contraction is contraction with no movement. In yoga when we stay in a pose we are engaging in isometric contraction. Eccentric contraction refers to a muscles contracting while lengthening. During yoga we create long and strong muscles by employing positions that favor eccentric contraction. This leads to more space in the joints. Short and strong muscles may compress the joints.

Working with the Body
The sensory and motor areas in the cerebral cortex, along with the basal ganglia, the visual and vestibular systems, and the cerebellum all modulate movement consciously or unconsciously. The spine has a series of stretch reflexes. Increasing strength and flexibility is accomplished by working with the stretch reflexes and training the interactions among these various brain areas. When feedback is diseased or damaged, the result may be tremor at rest or during movement, muscle spasm, and/or a general inability to coordinate muscle activity. Examples of diseases effecting motor control are Parkinson's, Huntington 's disease (Woody Guthrie disease), and ALS.

Use the Bio-Mechanics of the Body
1. Reciprocal inhibition: Engaging a muscle actively inhibits the opposing muscle, the antagonist, which can then be more effectively stretched.
2. Repetition: After coming out of a pose, the nervous system will integrate its bio - mechanics and more efficiently re-create the pose during the repetition.
3. Educate Muscle Spindles: The muscle spindle reflex detects changes in length and signals contraction to protect the muscle belly from tearing. By approaching a pose, backing off to a less intense stretch, and then reengaging in the stretch, the memory of length can increase.
4. Educate Golgi Tendon Organs: The Golgi tendon organ detects changes in load and signals the release of a muscle to protect the tendon; it overrides the muscle spindle reflex. Slow stretching can bypass the protective function and re-set the release point. The force applied during eccentric contraction also stimulates the Golgi tendon organs to release the muscle.

5. Facilitated Stretch: Proprioceptive Neuro-muscular Facilitating (PNF) is a method that acclimates a muscle spindle to new length. The sequence is: lengthen, then engage in an isometric contraction, then pause, then finally deepen the stretch. The timing is important: engage, pause, stretch in a ratio of 9:2:12 seconds. Caution should be exercised when muscle tone is low; ligaments could be stretched if the protective function of a contracting muscle is bypassed.

Stretching Techniques

1. Moving

Ballistic/elastic	– Not very useful, triggers stretch reflex
Dynamic	– Slow and controlled with repetition – Go until the muscle is fatigued. Tired muscles will be less elastic and will create a short muscle memory
Static/active	– Time held depends on strength of prime mover; e.g. holding leg up trains opposing muscles to work together

2. Non-moving – best preceded by dynamic stretching

Passive/static	– Relaxed, good for a cool down
Isometric	– Fastest way to increase flexibility and strength in tense muscles – Resistance is applied away from the direction of movement (contraindication: growing bones). – Assume position of passive stretch and tense the stretched muscle. Hold 7-15 sec. And release 20 sec.

3. Proprioceptive Neuromuscular Facilitating (PNF)
PNF takes full advantage of the fact that a contraction is turned off after an isometric stretch. This is the optimum time to acclimate the stretch receptors to a new muscle length.

PNF procedure 1:
→ Assume position of passive stretch.
→ Isometrically tense the stretched muscle for 7-15 sec.
→ Relax the muscle for 2-3 sec.
→ Increase passive stretch and hold 10-15 sec.
→ Relax 20 sec.

PNF procedure 2:
   → Assume passive stretch position
   → Contract the stretched muscle isometrically for 7-15 sec.
   → Contract the antagonist isometrically for 7-15 sec.
   → Relax 20 sec.

A series of yoga postures can take advantage of the fatigue that sets into a contracted muscle after about 9 seconds. Throughout the sequencing after a muscle is used, it is then in a position where it can be stretched more deeply. With conscious awareness of the preferred timing of the nervous system, we can maximize the value of the fatigue of the muscle. We stop just short of fatigue. Fatigue is not useful for creating a new state of muscle activity.

ASSIMILATION

Content

➢ Name the five sheaths of the koshas

➢ What are Farhi's seven moving principles?

➢ Define proprioception and resistance in terms of anatomy and describe why these are both important for our understanding of stretching.

➢ What kind of connective tissue effectively stretches?

Contemplation

➢ If yoga is a method to remove suffering, what makes us suffer?

➢ Which two of Farhi's moving principles speak to you?

➢ If, during yoga warm-ups, we choose to simply heat the body, what are we failing to address?

➢ How much freedom of movement do you want your joints to have?

➢ Does body awareness assist stretching?

➢ What are some factors that might influence range of motion from person to person, or day to day?

Personal Practice

➢ Initiate a time and place for practice and begin.

➢ Include body postures, movement, breathing and quiet time for meditation.

➢ Why is personal practice important for a yoga teacher?

Poses

➢ Begin developing facility with stick figures so you have a short-hand style for writing sequences for yourself and to hand to others.

➢ Draw 4 warm-ups that work for you and that you wish to share with others.

Where one knows that infinite happiness which can be grasped
by the intellect but is beyond the grasp of the senses,
wherein established one swerves not from that condition.
Bhagavad Gita 6/21

Chapter Two – Knowledge

SS 2- 3 Eight Root Causes and Sixteen Modifications

The story of the second chapter: how we become free from suffering is by knowledge. What we know defines how we think and behave. If we believe our attachments and identifications outside ourselves will complete us, we will incessantly demand that our environment conform to our will. If we believe an internal connection independent of all fluctuations of energy is our home and refuge, then we have a differing orientation. The transition is not quick. It requires re-thinking our assumptions. So, in this chapter we look at each piece of energy and the energy systems according to yoga and let our seer be the enjoyer. Chakras are situated along the spine. How do we move and breathe in hatha yoga practice to activate and support the energy along the spine? How does that experience of energy in the place of the body help free us from outer attachments?

Contents

---

[1] Practicum sections entitled "Keep it Simple" were written by Michelle Barnette.

*The ending of the modes and fluctuations of the chitta
occurs by practice and non-attachment.
Yoga Sutras I/12*

PHILOSOPHY

Samkhya Sutra 2: Eight Root Causes

Our assumptions about who we are and how we make ourselves happy are addressed in the opening sutras. The invitation is to see the complexities of energy and ultimately to comprehend that consciousness exists independent of all fluctuations of energy.

Eight root causes of nature: Pure Energy, Intellect, Ego and the Five Subtle Elements

After stating that we can be free of suffering, Kapil describes nature.

Nature expresses in eight stages:

1. Unmanifest Pure Energy
2. Intellect
3. Ego
4. Hearing   *(Space)*
5. Touch   *(Air)*
6. Sight   *(Fire)*
7. Taste   *(Water)*
8. Smell   *(Earth)*

Nature projects into life from the causal unmanifest, through subtle expression to gross matter. The first eight are causal and subtle. The subtle elements will transform into gross elements creating a universe that ranges from rarified space to congealed matter. Sound, language, and music, all related with space, are ephemeral compared with the grosser experiences of energy as matter, such as the buildings we inhabit and the food, clothing, and tools we use. Subtler experiences are related with perception, interpretation, and logic. When we meditate, by simply closing our eyes and sitting still, we let go of the gross experience of matter and attend to our subtler instruments. In the beginning stages of practice, when we move to the subtler realms, we gradually become more aware of awareness and consciousness as independent of experience.

The Koshas and the Eight-limbed Path

As we develop skill in moving inward, our experience teaches us that when our awareness is more subtle, we find more freedom inside. The grosser our attachments, the more we suffer.

Here are the two maps of energy from Samkhya and the koshas.

Samkhya	Koshas	
Causal: Self	Anandamayakosha	Bliss sheath
Subtle: Intelligence Ego and Mind Senses	Vijnanamayakosha[2] Manomayakosha Pranamayakosha	Knowledge sheath Mind sheath Breath sheath
Gross: Body	Annamayakosha	Food sheath

The Eight-Limbed Path – Ashtanga Yoga

In Patanjali's Yoga Sutras the path outlined for all types of seekers is called the eight-limbed path (Y.S. II/29). Its limbs correspond with the inward gradation of energy from gross to causal that we find in Samkhya and in the theory of the koshas.

Yama	In relationship to society: the great vows of non-violence, truthfulness, non-stealing, control of energy, and non-accumulation	
Niyama	In relationship to oneself: personal observances of purity, contentment, austerity, self-study, and surrender	
Asana	Posture	Body
Pranayama	Breathing exercises	Senses
Pratyahar	Inward turning	Mind
Dharana	Concentration	Mind & ego
Dhyana	Meditation	Ego
Samadhi	Absorption	Intelligence & bliss

[2] *Vijnanamayakosha* is pronounced *Vigyanamayakosha.* When the letter "j" and "n" are paired as "jn," the pronunciation is "gy."

The training of yoga cultivates sheaths as valuable instruments rather than hindrances to our happiness and service. The value of our training is that we eventually clear the coverings of the intellect[3] and live in the light of our intelligence consciousness, realizing intimacy and connection with life through our awareness.

> *When the mind runs after the wandering senses,*
> *Then it carries away one's understanding*
> *as the wind carries away a ship on the waters.*
> *Bhagavad Gita 2/67*

Samkhya Sutra 3: Sixteen Modifications

The Senses

Most of us assume that our body and senses define who we are. The senses move among the objects of senses. The mind perceives through the senses and is organized by the ego. The ego evaluates experience. The intellect guides the experience and our responses to the environment. However, Yoga philosophy states that all experiences are painful or neutral.[4] All pleasure ends in loss. No experience in the world of change can be sustained. It will end. Therein lies the root of suffering: attachment to what ends in loss. The challenge of yoga is to look beyond our ordinary means of defining ourselves and gaining happiness.

The sixteen modifications of nature are the cognitive and active senses, the mind and the primordial elements. The mind is attached to the gross world through senses and acts to obtain the objects of the senses. This teaching is daunting to beginners of Samkhya. However, the teaching correlates so neatly with modern science that overlooking the details of this teaching is a disservice to Samkhya and Yoga. The senses are windows of perception in the body that open to the world around us. Our mind perceives through information gained from all five senses – hearing, touch, sight, taste, and smell. According to neuro-anatomy, each sense organ is a discrete and refined translator of energy from the environment into perception. The mechanisms by which we receive information from the world via the organs of the senses, and the way in which we perceive the world in the association cortices[5] of the brain, are two distinct functions of the nervous system. Without perception, the senses have no value. Without the senses, perception cannot function.

---

[3] Intellect is *chitta* in Yoga philosophy and *buddhi* in Sāmkhya philosophy. It is the place in us where the light of consciousness manifests and enlivens.

[4] *Klista* or *aklista*. Y.S. I/5.

[5] Cortices = plural for cortex. The cerebral cortex is the outermost part of the brain that is the seat of cognition and creativity. It is subdivided into four areas of specialized function.

The five primordial elements are simplistic, but they correlate with our senses and perception, thus they are useful for our yogic research into consciousness. The value of this cosmology[6] is to comprehend our experience of diversity outside the body and align it with our experience within the body. The macrocosm of the vast world around us can be understood and navigated by comprehending the microcosm of our limited body. One way to contemplate the contiguous nature of outer to inner is through light: the existence of light as an element outside of us, the reception of light by the eyes, and the perception of light in the brain are three aspects of the same experience.

The primordial element of fire includes the properties of light, heat, and power. The experience of light as heat and power is felt as heat in the body. From science, we know that our metabolism is dependent on carbon chain fuel that captures solar energy. The same power of heat digests food through mechanical and bio-chemical process that then makes energy available for heat within the body. The food also provides energy, and with the energy we can perceive light. By contemplating in this way, we can realize the principles of this philosophy, a living philosophy. When we see how these universal principles function, we can witness nature more and identify less.

According to yoga, if we can quiet the senses, the mind can quiet. The mind has the capacity to withdraw from the stimulation of the objects of senses. When we move into the life around us, we move from subtler to grosser instruments. When we practice, we reverse the process and move from gross to subtle. Our consciousness is always the same. It is watching the movement both ways. When we move to the subtler realms we move from awareness of material objects to awareness of subtle energy. From there, our consciousness merges back into a field of pure energy. Then we can realize the self as seer – independent and stable under all circumstances.

He who is without attachment on all sides, encountering this or that, pleasant or
unpleasant, neither rejoicing nor disliking his wisdom stands firm.
And when he withdraws the senses completely from the objects of the senses,
as a tortoise withdraws its limbs into his shell, his wisdom stands firm.
Bhagavad Gita 2/57-58

---

[6] The primordial elements of this ancient system are similar to the Chinese system that includes water, fire, air, earth, wood, and metal. The Chinese model is not hierarchical; it is visualized as a star pattern of seasons and interactions.

To praise the sun is to praise our own eyes.
We are the mirror as well as the face in it.
Rumi

The Chakra System

The Chakras

Chakra theory comes from a branch of yoga called Tantra.[7] The knowledge of Tantra is ancient, and it reemerged during a medieval revival in India in the 12th–17th Centuries A.C.E. This teaching along with the inspiration of ecstatic poets and visionaries such as Kabir in the fifteenth century[8] encouraged practice and direct knowledge of truth, throwing off the dulling dominance of the priest classes. The knowledge of the chakras can inspire research into our own experience of the projection of nature and energy.

Table of Senses, Organs of Sense, and Elements, from Subtle to Gross
With Corresponding Chakras

Cognitive sense	Organ of sense	Element as media	Chakras
Hearing	Ears	Space	vishuddha
Touch	Skin	Air	anahata
Sight	Eyes	Fire / Light	manipura
Taste	Tongue	Water / Liquid	svadhishthana
Smell	Nose	Earth	muladhara

Beyond the Senses – An Expanded Vision

When the senses are tamed, then we can have a vision of the whole. Each sense gives only a partial glimpse. Our consciousness is shining through all. What we seek is shining by the function of the senses yet freed from the senses. As we place more value on ourselves as the home of experience, chakra theory gives us a way to explore that home. This table is a template for that exploration.

---

[7] *The Art of Tantra*, Philip Rawson.
[8] *The Kabir Book*, Robert Bly.

Table of Chakras, Neuro-endocrine Function, Location in Body, and Related Emotion/Experience

Chakra	Neuro-endocrine	Location	Emotion/Experience
Brahma*	unknown	Above head	Bliss
Ajna	Pituitary/Pineal	Above sinus bones in brain	Peace
Lalana	unknown	Palate of mouth	Mental stability
Vishuddha	Thyroid/Parathyroid	Base of throat	Contained expression
Anahata	Arterial/Thymus	Heart	Grief
Manipura	Adrenals/Pancreas	Solar plexus	Anger
Svadhishthana	Sex glands	Area of sexual glands	Desire
Muladhara	unknown	Coccygeal body	Fear

* The brahma chakra corresponds with intellect, chitta and buddhi.

Emotions

The senses give us information, and we form responses to that information. Our emotions are powerful responses to the environment. Emotions are adaptive. Without the powerful emotional response of fear, one would not jump out of the way of an on-coming car. The emotion of fear jolts the body into action. We might also be angry after jumping out of the way. When we are angry, we have the energy to assess the situation and see what else might be done. Do we need to keep running? Do we need to make a police report?

We have three fundamental emotions: fear, anger and grief. When considering these, we are thinking only of the body and its needs for survival and homeostasis.[9] Love is often considered an emotion, but in this philosophy, love is not of the body – it is a quality of the soul. Fear, anger and grief are powerful and adaptive emotions that disturb the normal flow of joy that comes from the self. They are like three primary colors, and emotions such as shame, guilt, or disappointment can be explored as a combination or tone of the three primary ones. Fear is felt low in the body. We use our legs to run when we are afraid. Under extremely fearful conditions, the body urinates and evacuates. Anger is felt in the center of the body. With anger we have energy to fight. The adrenal glands are involved in giving us sustained energy. There is a relationship between anger and our vision. "Blind anger" is a term for that experience. Or, "I am so angry, I see red." Grief is felt in the chest as a kind of heaving and dissolving. Research on grieving indicates that as a result of grief, the physiology shifts back to homeostasis.[10]

---

[9] Homeostasis, covered in greater detail in later chapters, is a state of physiological equilibrium produced by a balance of functions and of chemical composition within an organism.

[10] *American Journal of Psychiatry*, "CLOC Research," University of Michigan, and "Functional Neuroanatomy of Grief."

Emotion is out of balance when it is out of proportion to experience, either depleted or exaggerated. Not feeling a feeling or becoming overwhelmed by a feeling make emotion maladaptive.

The lower centers carry more value for survival. Psychologist Abraham Maslow's "hierarchy of needs" correlates with the centers along the spine. Fear is an experience that helps us survive. First we need a place to stay and food to eat. Once we have gained basic security, we climb the ladder of needs. Belonging comes next. The needs of the heart take precedence after we feel safe. Our intellectual needs come after the other needs are settled. If our lunch is late and we are angry with the waiter, we may think our reaction is inappropriate. That is an intellectual decision. The body has made another choice. It is certain that the need for food should be fulfilled immediately. That more basic need comes from lower in the body. We can observe our reaction, and then choose to use anger or humor. If we are well fed, the situation is not critical. If we starve all the time, we will use our anger energy to secure food more regularly. If we are well fed, we can afford to browse in a bookstore after we eat.

Environment

The value of learning to observe the areas of the chakras is that we begin to understand our relationship to our environment. How do we respond? How does everyone respond? We are part of experience. In yoga, we experience and we watch experience. We are the knower and the known. We watch our reactions. We are not interested in repression or suppression. In the name of being loving and truthful, we do not want to inhibit a natural emotion that may seem against our will, or not appropriate. What yoga adds to the experience of emotion is learning to observe it deeply and then to decide how it is serving us.

Anger, an emotion that many of us suppress in the name of not harming others, is extraordinarily useful and full of information. The idea is to allow yourself to feel and see that you are angry by accessing your deepest seer. By accessing the seer, you may understand your anger by listening closely to your speech and hearing it in your word choice or tone. Then the goal is not to suppress or express the anger. Feel it. It is difficult. See what information you gain from the experience. The temptation is to feel that we are "right" because we are angry. Our position is not necessarily right, but most certainly something needed to be "righted," and anger is good information. The emotion is full of sensation, energy, and information.

What results from anger is clarity, and a need to make a distinct choice. First comes confusion, and then maybe some grief as you "let go" of needing to express it. Then clarity and insight come. Usually our insight is regarding the need for protection. Where do boundaries need to come into place? With whom do I need to negotiate? How can I approach this?

The human experience is intense and complex. Eliminating emotion from our experience does not work. We cannot cut ourselves off from our experience and remain authentic human beings. The energetic intensity of being human is intimate to endocrine function and the central nervous system. Endocrine glands do not operate independently. So much of our response to the environment can be tracked in subtle pathways through feedback loops and into shifts in our internal environment. Our glands use the blood stream for transportation. The nervous system provides immediate reactions and observations. There are many ways that the molecules of the body communicate. We gain broad brushstrokes of information when we react intensely. The big picture shows up in intense internal states of feeling.

We can refine our experience and our thinking. This is human culture, a process of refinement. When I was having trouble containing my emotions, I asked my teacher what I should do. "Refine your emotion into devotion," he answered. "Think and meditate. Concentrate your energy and make it one-pointed. Settle your thoughts. Gradually you will begin to feel that the heart can be devoted to your work."

Chakras and Imagery

The chakras are mysterious.[11] We do not have enough information to have a complete theory because the information comes in subtle states of awareness and in meditation, not through any objective means. The chakras are often called "yoga anatomy." I prefer that the term anatomy refer to gross anatomy. The chakras are the subtle experiences of a gross event called the living body.

Images are part of our human experience. C.G. Jung has defined symbols as images whose meaning cannot be defined. The emotional and intellectual depth of a powerful symbol goes beyond our ability to reduce into one meaning.[12] Images and symbols have held value throughout human history.[13] Jung suggested that the most valuable way to find meaning in our personal lives would be to attend to our own image-making function through dreams, symbols, and "active imagination."[14] From the rich life of the symbol we can orient our modern "psyche" to the difficulties of living in a new era where the value of symbols to hold our search for the "numinous" has fallen beyond our conscious cultural agreement. The numinous refers to what is mysterious or awe-inspiring. The root of the word "numen" means to nod. The numinous is what inspires us to bow. Useful symbols remind us to bow to what is larger than ourselves.

---

[11] *Anatomy of the Spirit*, Carolyn Myss.

[12] *Number and Time*, Marie-Louise von Franz.

[13] *The New God-Image*: A study of Jung's Key Letters Concerning the Evolution of the Western God Image, Edward F. Edinger.

[14] *Anatomy of the Psyche*: Alchemical Symbolism in Psychotherapy, Edward F. Edinger.

Kundalini Yoga

Anyone who has ever dreamed at night knows that image-making is beyond our control.[15] Images show up. If we attend to them, they become a kind of language. As we explore the locations of the chakras, subtle experiences are "seen" and experienced. Additionally, Swami Bawra taught that focusing on any center along the spine assists concentration, and images may show up that assist concentration. All centers bring their own satisfaction. Focusing on the higher centers assists meditation.

Literature on kundalini yoga was illustrated with flower petals as chakras and with a coiled serpent at the base of the spine. The symbol of the serpent represents energy.[16] The image of the serpent traditionally inspires fear; here it indicates energy trapped in the lower centers. The ascending movement that occurs when the energy is released is like the movement of the serpent. In the theory of kundalini yoga, the upward movement of energy stored at the base of the spine[17] takes us beyond fear. Fear is a response to a threat to our physical well-being. As the prana moves from the base of the spine toward the head, we move beyond attachment to the physical body into subtle and causal energetic experience. We know that we are not just the physical body. We become free of the fear of death.

Energy in the Body

The sites of the chakras in the body hold intensity. The crown of the head, the brahma chakra, has the most power. It is called the "thousand-petaled lotus." The ajna chakra between the eyes is next in power and intensity. It is depicted as two petals, representing the ida and pingala, the twin lines of force that interweave like two snakes and cross at each of the chakras. These twin lines of force are activated by the breath from the two nostrils, the right nostril activates the ida and the left, the pingala. When these two are in balance, the body is healthy and the mind is calm. Below the ajna chakra, varying numbers of petals indicate each chakra. The base chakra of earth has four petals, a cross-cultural indication of earth energy.

The movement of energy in the body has a system. Like all life, it expresses with order and intelligence. We are familiar with how the energy of electricity is distributed in our communities. Power plants harness electricity from fuel or power such as water. Electricity then travels across miles of territory in high-tension wires to transformer stations. Transformer stations are sprinkled in neighborhoods and cities. In those, the energy is reduced to a lower voltage so it can be safely used. The chakra system is an energy distribution system. The chakras are transformers. Kundalini yoga's term for the

---

[15] In his book, *The Body of Myth: Mythology,* Shamanic Trance, and the Sacred Geology of the Body, J. Nigro Sansonese explores the interface between the experience of the body and the image-making function of the brain.

[16] The serpent is the traditional symbol for the healing power of Western medicine: the caduceus is of two snakes interweaving around a staff.

[17] The movement down the body goes through two interweaving channels, the *ida* and *pingala*. The ascending movement goes through a central channel in the spine called the *shushumna*.

reversal of that energy, as if back to the power station, is sushumna, the flow of energy up the spine and into the head which brings absorption into the source of energy and consciousness.

Summary

In meditation and in the poses, when we become aware of these centers, we have the opportunity to internally resolve our experience. Our goal in yoga is to hold experience in a more balanced way. When we come into deep relaxation in the body, we have the opportunity to contain our experience of the world. Thus the desire of the sexual center can be transformed into feeling connected with others without needing another person for comfort. The fear we may feel can be embraced and understood as a need for security that we can provide by living well in the body. These kinds of experiences come naturally as a result of practice.

- *Eyes quiet thought*
- *Food quiets the tongue*
- *Heart quiets the feelings*
- *Feeling powerful quiets the need for power*
- *Sexual contact quiets the need for connection*
- *Excretion quiets the base*

Our goal in yoga practice is to rely on our knowledge and our practice. Reliance on doctors, research, teachers, experts, and gurus is a stepping-stone to finding the truth for ourselves. Indirect knowledge is what we gain from others. Direct knowledge is what we seek. My guru would say, "If I point to the sun and say it exists, it is not enough to believe me. You must try to see the sun with your own eyes."

There is yogic practice of using sound with each center. The sounds are called bij mantras, meaning seed sounds. Repeating the sound while visualizing the center can stimulate and create satisfaction within the center, thereby helping us find balance within ourselves and our responsibilities.

Chakras and Mantras

Site	Element	Color	Sound
Root	Earth	Red	Lung
Sex center	Water	Orange	Vung
Solar plexus	Fire	Yellow	Rung
Heart	Air	Green	Yung
Throat	Space	Blue	Hung
Palate		Blue	Aum
Between brows		Indigo	Aum
Crown		White	Aum

Work in the Chakras requires "holding paradox" and "witnessing the pause."

Maturity in yoga and in life is understanding paradox: contradictions that do not resolve. For instance, we strive to live in a healthy manner and then we die. No one can resolve this apparent contradiction. Working with the chakras can help us manage paradox.

> ➢ In the earth center, how can we breathe non-judgment into the processes of fearing and belonging? (smell, red, memory, defense)

> ➢ In the water center, how can we flow with relationships and not get overwhelmed by the undertow of needs? How can we breathe non-judgment into family and relationships? (taste, orange, sexuality, relationships)

> ➢ In the fire center, how can we be powerful but not egotistical?
> (sight, yellow, personal power)

> ➢ In the air center, how can we love in all it vastness and still have boundaries? (touch, green, dawning of unity)

> ➢ In space, how can we speak and influence without disrespecting the space of others? (blue, hearing, purification)

> ➢ At the palate, how can we hold the mind stable while attending fully to the world around us?

> ➢ Between the eyes, how do we hold the pure I-am as both definition of self and freedom from limitation? (indigo, witness, freedom, knowing, I-amness)

> ➢ In the crown chakra, how, why, and to what do we surrender?
> (white, peace-beyond-understanding, the all)

TECHNIQUE

Yoga Therapy

What makes yoga therapeutic is the approach of the techniques of asana and pranayama and the inclusion of all the *koshas*. Yoga therapy aims toward the needs of the student. As such, yoga therapy is more complex than teaching a set series of poses because the needs of the student exist on all *koshas* of body, breath, mind, and wisdom. A good therapeutic class will provide enough possibility for exploration that the students can meet their own needs within what is presented. In other words, there is enough good alignment, enough careful instruction around breath and opening areas that restrict breath, enough pauses and focus for the mind, and enough silence for awareness to be considered that the students can naturally seek their own level of work. Respecting all *koshas* and allowing them to be present is the value of yoga therapy.

Adult as Learner
Adults continually develop skills driven by their curiosity and a need for self-mastery. To support their search for ways to adapt to shifting challenges and responsibilities, we provide details to the practices. As teachers, we constantly scour our own practice and keep a keen eye on the horizon of possibility for serving the adoption of what is valuable and diminishing any hindrances to our wholeness and well-being.

Philosophy
The purpose of yoga practice is to remove suffering. Practice that encourages craving, attachment, and egoism does not free us from our limitations.

Technique
Technique is not a mechanical application of knowledge; it is seeking homeostasis through a fluctuating system. Time of day, different foods we have eaten, and how hard we have worked both mentally and physically all impact our practice and create conditions that will necessarily be addressed during asana. Asana practice is adapted to meet specific goals. Although each pose and breathing practice has its individual integrity, practice will always vary. We look for possibilities, probabilities, and interrelationships. The order of a system is found within consciousness, not the technique itself. The whole of our practice is enfolded within each part. Continuity of awareness creates a therapeutic environment that is more holistic than specific. In our practice we do not look merely for a specific cure for any dysfunction. Healing is as much mental as physical. The value of technique lies in its ability to open our awareness to the value of the life force moving as breath and health and to create mental stability.

Alignment is agreement.
Donna Farhi

Variation breeds attention.
Desikachar

Alignment and Sequencing

Alignment is key; then sequencing. We learn both as we progress, but favor alignment first. From appropriate alignment in key poses, the heightened body awareness will assist your understanding of the value of appropriate sequencing. Gradually, as your knowledge of anatomy increases, you will appreciate and begin to amplify the value of sequencing.

Alignment is the appropriate activation of muscle groups to maximize the space in the joints. When there is length in the active muscles and strength to maintain the alignment, then the body experiences more energy and greater longevity. Overuse of certain muscles results in compression of the joints, greater wear and tear, restricted circulation, and less energy.

Sequencing is an art based on the knowledge and experience of the body that creates the conditions for healthy alignment. Sequencing includes both warm-ups and the series of asanas. Two maxims of sequencing are...

| *Activate before release.* | *When lengthened, strengthen.* |

Memory of length in the muscles is carried by the muscle spindles in the muscle bellies and Golgi tendon receptors in the tendons (more detail in Chapter 6). When muscles are long and strong, rather than contracted and strong, it is called "flexibility."

When we work with one asana we can vary many elements:
- *Breath Rhythm*
- *Preparation for the pose*
- *Sphere of attention (the focus)*

First we respect the virtue of the pose, its integrity and its relationship to gravity, and then we enliven the pose with variation, seeking to find the life or the prana of the pose.

Resistance has value
Recognize, honor, and use resistance. It highlights where we need to work and protects our weaknesses.
- *Work on the edge, and create variations around it.*
- *Adaptations and modifications reduce resistance.*

Use the Bio-Mechanics of the Body: Concentric and Eccentric Contractions

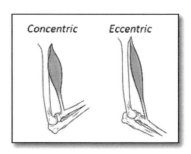

There are two kinds of muscle contractions:
- → Concentric where the muscle belly shortens
- → Eccentric where the muscle belly is lengthened while engaged

A bicep muscle in concentric contraction shortens and folds the arm at the elbow. A bicep in eccentric contraction engages at arm's length to resist pressure, such as holding out a tray or pushing a car. During yoga postures we often lengthen a muscle and then use it. This creates long and strong muscles that support flexibility and full range of motion.

The nervous system assists the bio-mechanics of stretching. Our understanding highlights effective stretching.

Reciprocal inhibition: Engaging a muscle actively inhibits the opposing muscle, the antagonist, which can then be more effectively stretched. For example, in downward facing dog pose, engage quadriceps to inhibit hamstrings, which then lengthen. The most effective stretch is not passive, but active. Once the hamstrings are lengthened, engage them in eccentric contraction, which pulls the hips back over the heels. (Refer to Chapter 3 for more details and diagram.)

Repetition: After coming out of a pose, the nervous system will integrate the bio-mechanics and more efficiently recreate the pose during the repetition.

Educate Muscle Spindles: The muscle spindle reflex detects changes in length and signals contraction to protect the muscle belly from tearing. By approaching a pose, backing off to a less intense stretch, and then reengaging in the stretch, the memory of length can increase.

Educate Golgi Tendon Organs: The Golgi tendon organ detects changes in load and signals the release of a muscle to protect the tendon; it overrides the muscle spindle reflex. Slow stretching can bypass the protective function and re-set the release point. The force applied during eccentric contraction can also stimulate the Golgi tendon organs to release the muscle belly.

Facilitated Stretch: Proprioceptive Neuro-muscular Facilitating (PNF) is a method that acclimatizes a muscle spindle to new length. The sequence is:

Lengthen	Isometric contraction	Pause	Deepen the stretch

The timing is important – contraction: pause: stretch in a ratio of 7(-14): 2: 9 seconds. Caution should be exercised when muscle tone is low; ligaments could be stretched if the protective function of a contracting muscle is bypassed.

The Aim of Asana Practice

The heart of yoga is to craft an experience that is *sthira sukha*, stable and easy.[18]

- Respect the classical asana. Know its basic value. Find the ground of each pose. Gravity is a friend.

- Observe areas where the spine and the pose lose their integrity due to tension, which is experienced as resistance. If the tension does not release in the pose, the spine and pose lose integrity. Spinal integrity is often the neutral spine, one that includes the natural curves of the spine. In other poses the embryonic "C" shape may be intended.

- Because of the proximity of breath to spine, the oscillation of breath brings awareness to the shape of the spine.

- Breath and movement: natural integration of mind and body occur when breath is synchronized with movement.

- Breath is the intelligence of the body: conscious breathing heightens awareness.

  - → Initially: asana deepens breath.
  - → Then: asana releases tensions and the posture develops a fuller breath.
  - → Finally: breath awareness can be sustained.

- *Vinyasa*: a method of asana practice where one repeats going into and out of poses in sequence with breath. The value is that the nervous system learns by repetition, the connective tissue is warmed, and the muscle spindles can lengthen appropriately. *Vinyasa krama* means gradual and repeated movement to release resistance. The sequence is appropriate to the resistance.

- *Pratikriyasana*: a counterpose balances the effects of previous poses. Poses can leave unknown physiological effects over time. The Sanskrit term *pratikriyasana* means "against the action of asana." Balanced sequences include counterposes that mitigate any strain.

- Include some dynamic breath/posture sequence as part of every session. Value movement and value staying in the pose.

---

[18] The material of this technique section is indebted to the work of Desikachar in The Heart of Yoga, and Mohan's, Yoga for Body, Breath and Mind.

Elegant Sequencing

Effective sequencing has an intentional arc that heightens body awareness, effectively uses variations, takes resistance into account, and works with the release mechanisms of the body to create change. Efficient change includes engaging a muscle before stretching, stretching it while lengthened, and engaging it while lengthened in eccentric contraction. We then return to a more normal concentric contraction.

Variations with *Janushirshasana*
Seated with left leg folded into the opposite thigh.

A. Bow over folded leg   Bow between knees

Awareness of base is different in both positions – note how.

B. Spinal twist to left   Then right

Awareness of spine is different in both positions – note how.

C. Left arm up, push off with right   Extend forward

With awareness of   Push right hand back into earth
base and spine.   Use abdominal core while engaging
                                           extended leg. Hold 7-14 seconds.

D. Release out and place hands back   Lift hips

Note what muscles are engaging that had been lengthening.

Repeat: C. Extend forward
From holding, release spine forward with left hand crossing the shin.
Continue to engage quadriceps of extended leg, pressing heel down.

Note what areas release in the back. Note how the right hand pressing down on the ground assists the orientation of the spine.

E. Complete *Janushirshasana* with two arms forward. Increase breath awareness in the pose to assist the length of the lumbar region. The inhalation brings awareness to the length and shape of the spine. The exhalation assists extension.

Release out and pause with the eyes closed to feel the effects.

The Most Fundamental Movement is Breath

Our natural breathing pattern is our starting point. Each individual will have a different shape to their breath and will gradually develop a more complete natural breath as tension, habits, and connective tissue shift.

Breath is a mover: breath takes form into function. Naturally the body exhales more deeply on a forward fold. Inhaling into the chest on a backbend opens the thoracic spine.

Breath should be *dirgha*, long and steady, and *sukshma*, smooth and subtle. The medulla (hindbrain) controls the involuntary breath. When breath is voluntary it stimulates the reticular formation in the hindbrain, which increases alertness and stimulates cranial nerves, that is, aspects of the parasympathetic nervous system.[19] A slowed, voluntary breath creates sustained attention, and links mind with body. Within a larger field of attention, a pose will have more comprehensive value.

The exhalation is the area of exploration in yoga that increases value and interest. With the exhalation, the body releases tension and finds extension. The exhalation helps to lengthen muscles groups, stabilize the pose, and create awareness with intention.

The inhalation brings energy and awareness. The inhalation is created with muscular contraction and can enhance extension with eccentric contraction, that is, one can create strength with flexibility by contracting a muscle when it is lengthened.

The breath gives feedback on the pose. Breathing creates movement in the pose that provides information. Adaptation results. Additionally, movement of the body impacts breathing. One informs the other: movement↔breath and breath↔movement. Breathe fully in the poses; a faltering or shortened breath signals a need to modify the pose.

Synchronized movement with breath intensifies practice by focusing the mind. This frees the ego to experience without attachment. Attachment to outcome is bondage. Attachment to breath is yoga practice. Breath preceding movement is preferred as it encourages more fluid action.

> *Summary: Poses teach breathing. Breathing teaches poses.*

---

[19] The relaxation division of the autonomic nervous system.

PRACTICUM

Keep it Simple: Skillful Communication

- Be clear: Specific and concise (Good Father)
  - → Say the pose
  - → Say the breath
  - → Give 3 cues
- Emulate compassion in your voice (Good Mother)
  - → Let your students know you care
- Emulate confidence in your voice:
  - → Your students want to feel taken care of
  - → Put them at ease
- Let your voice match the feeling you want to evoke
  - → When should your voice be uplifting?
  - → When should your voice be strong?
  - → When should your voice be soft?
- Be ok with silence. Insight occurs here.
  - → Listen and look. Do not miss out on the opportunity to learn from your students.
- Be honest (SATYA)
  - → Teach only what you yourself have experienced, know and believe
- Know the pose so well that you can invent creative ways to teach it

WORD CHOICE/ACTIVITY

- ➢ Brainstorm words for:

  - − Lift:

  - − Hold:

  - − Release:

A FEW THINGS TO CONSIDER:
- Don't use "don't"
- Minimize gerunds ("-ing" words, such as lifting, stepping, extending, etc.)
- Become aware of your own personal teaching "tics" (words you overuse in instruction, for example, "gently twist and gently close the eyes")
- Give instruction, but also give space / pause, time for students' own reflection

Bless the spine
for it is the whole story
Mary Oliver

ANATOMY

Musculoskeletal System

The musculoskeletal system functions in a mechanical fashion. The relationship between muscles and bones is like a drawbridge with a large elastic pull that shrinks to lift the bridge.

Muscles are controlled by the nervous system and their contraction stretches the connective tissue around the muscles. Excitation and inhibition are opposing processes that work together to create movement. Inhibition is an active process; it is not simply a lack of excitation. Without inhibition, movement would not occur.

The muscles are nourished and cleansed by arterial blood and venous return. The byproducts and waste matter from metabolism are also cleansed by the lymph system. The lymph system is part of the immune system.

Yoga facilitates the balance between strength and flexibility in the muscles of the body, which assists in realigning the joints of the skeleton.

Types of Muscle Tissue

Striated/skeletal muscle: Sometimes referred to as "voluntary." Creates movement and is under voluntary control.

Cardiac muscle: Found in the wall of the heart. Under autonomic control. The heart will continue to beat when separated from the body. Two heart cells will continue to beat in unison for a time when separated and, when reunited, will resume beating in unison. Yogis have shown conscious control of this muscle.

Smooth muscle: Sometimes referred to as "involuntary." Found in most internal organs. Yogis have been known to control involuntary muscle.

Mixed muscle: Diaphragm – mixed muscle is a combination of striated and smooth muscle; therefore, breathing can be voluntary or involuntary.

Getting to Know the Muscles

Muscles have different shapes; form and function correlate.

Muscles have bellies, and origins and insertions where they attach to the bones.

The names of the muscles often describe their shape, e.g. a bicep has two origins ("bi" means two), and quadratus lumborum ("quad" means four) is shaped like a rectangle.

Movement and Yoga

During voluntary movement, the contraction and relaxation of the striated muscles not only helps the body to pump blood back to the heart, the movement also helps the lymph to move back toward the area of the heart. The lymph system cleanses the tissues of waste products of metabolism and immune functions.

Voluntary muscles are contracted 10% at all times. This is called muscle tone. Yoga helps us to maintain this tone. Muscle tone is a state of firing of certain numbers of nerves at all times. Some are activated while others rest; they trade off so that one motor unit is not continually firing. Motor units are one nerve to 100 muscles fibers that fire in an "all or none" fashion. Excessive muscle tone consumes more muscle energy in the resting phase, compresses the blood supply, and accumulates waste.

Visceral muscle is massaged during practice. The stretch and release assists blood flow and elasticity.

Yoga develops control of the diaphragm. The conscious relationship with breath is a conscious link with practice that yogis carry around at all times.

Stretching releases muscle tension. Muscular tension can reduce the space in the joints leading to "wear and tear" damage and arthritis.

Stretching stimulates bone growth and bone density.

Muscles are vascular and stretching provides a "squeeze and soak" effect that brings an increased volume of blood into a muscle. Large numbers of mitochondria[20] in the muscles provide energy through metabolism. With an increase in blood flow and an oxygen rich environment, stretching increases the energy available for movement.

The close of a yoga class should include a warming down period when light movement encourages release of any muscular contractions incurred during class. Oxygen then circulates freely and waste products are removed.

Skeletal System

Bones, ligaments, and tendons are made up of connective tissue, all with varying degrees of elasticity. Bones are clearly the densest and have the most restricted movement, with tendons coming in a close second. Tendons have more tensile strength

---

[20] Mitochondria are powerhouses of the cell.

than bones. Tensile strength is the maximum stress a material can withstand while being stretched before failing. Under extreme stress, bones are more likely to break than tendons are to tear. Bones repair more easily. Bones are alive, porous, and filled with marrow that plays a key role in the blood supply. Bones change shape over time and with correct alignment, the shapes of the ends of bones that come to play in the joints can mutate to assist efficient movement. Bones, like all tissues, are dynamic, living structures.

The skeleton does not produce movement but makes movement possible. Movement takes place at the joints. Our bones act as levers that turn around the joints. Our skeleton protects the soft internal organs, including the brain.

The skeleton has two parts:

Axial skeleton	Skull, sacrum, vertebrae, ribs, sternum and hyoid bone. 80 bones. Fractures are more serious here. Less mobile.
Appendicular skeleton	Pectoral (clavicle, and scapula) and pelvic girdles, and the bones of the arms, forearms, wrists, hands, thigh, legs and feet. 126 bones. Fractures are more common here. More mobile.

Bone Structure
The outermost bone layer is like a sheath that weaves into other connective tissues of the body.

Compact bone provides support.

Cancellous bone is a latticed truss system capable of reorientation. This is the part of the bone that can change shape as the bones adjust their alignment. Here, the red marrow contains masses of developing and mature red and white blood cells, which pack the spaces between the trusses.

The medullary cavity (the center of a bone shaft, also known as the marrow cavity) lightens bone weight.

Getting to Know the Bones
As you look at the bones, examine how structure and function correlate.

The human hand has 25 joints and 58 movements.

The hands and feet contain more than half of the bones in the body.

Connective Tissue
Cartilage protects the ends of the bones and is the first area attacked by arthritis.

Cartilage is subject to damage due to repetitive movement and weight-bearing stress.

The bursae are synovial sacs that cushion the place where muscles, ligaments, or tendons make a sharp turn in the anatomical structure. These sacs help prevent wear and tear but when aggravated by poor posture and/or overuse they become inflamed, causing a condition called bursitis.

Ligaments are found in joints and function to hold bones together.

Tendons connect muscle to specific points on the bones (tuberosities).

Those Bones are Interesting
Bones make up 18% of our body weight and their tensile strength approximates that of iron.

Bones store reserve materials and in times of shortage (calcium), they are leached from the bones. Calcium is used by the nervous system. Exercise sends minerals back into the bones

Bones need oxygen, glucose, stress (exercise), and water. Yoga is an efficient method to feed the bones.

Blood flows through bone like sap in a tree.

Bones require some protein for maintenance but too much dietary protein creates a more acidic pH, which increases the demand for calcium which is then leached from the bones. Estrogen stimulates bone growth. Menopause is a challenging time for bone health.

Bones will conform to distortions in movement. Proper alignment in the poses changes the shape of bones.

Yoga postures stimulate bone matter from a maximum number of directions.

Conditions that Affect the Bones[21]
Osteoporosis: Loss of bone density. Gentle yoga is useful.

Osteoarthritis: Inflammation of the joints. Contributing factors are stress and the release of cortisol, poor posture, and poor circulation. Gentle yoga movement with breathing is helpful.

---

[21] For the most complete descriptions of conditions and treatment via poses see: *Back Care Basics*, by Mary Pullig Schatz, MD

<u>Rheumatoid Arthritis</u>: Arthritic degeneration due to autoimmune response. Gentle yoga movement with breathing is helpful.

<u>Spondylosis and Spondylolisthesis</u>: Connections between vertebrae weaken and break. Yoga provides muscular support for intervertebral joints.

<u>Injury</u>: Injuries result in the formation of scar tissue in and around joints, which restricts movement. The alignment and repetition of yoga poses releases scar tissue and helps the body regain a normal range of motion.

<u>Spinal injuries and disk problems</u>: Reducing compression and creating space is important. Not creating a worse problem is more important.

Concerns for Yoga Teachers
The base of the spine lies in the pelvic area called the ilia (singular, ilium). The fused vertebral area called the sacrum rests directly between two wide pelvic bones. The spine and hips are thus connected at the sacro-iliac joint, which is a problematic area during yoga practice. If this joint is over-stretched, tendons are lengthened (bone to muscle), ligaments between the bones are lengthened and the area becomes unstable, leading to further injury. This joint has little muscular support, nor is there much blood flow to assist healing.

Another area of concern in the hips and lower back is the sciatic nerve. Its point of origin is near lumbar vertebrae 4 & 5 and it courses under a rotator muscle behind the iliac crest called the piriformis. The sciatic nerve has a diameter approximately the size of the little finger. If it is impinged upon, it remains inflamed for about a month. During that time, avoiding re-inflammation is critical. With sciatic pain, the hip and entire leg are subject to numbing and/or pain. To correct the condition, time and patience are required, and yoga can help. Poses that continue to inflame the area should be discontinued. This proves difficult because a forward bend is the intuitive response to back pain and is the worst choice for relief from sciatica, since it aggravates the nerve.

Beginning with the Spine

The top vertebra of the spinal column is the atlas. It articulates with the skull. The occipital bone rests on the atlas. One cannot palpate cervical vertebrae 1 & 2 since they have no spinous processes. The top of the spine is at about the level of the temporomandibular joint. The position of the jaw and chin alter the shape of the neck and upper spine.

The spine is made up of 33 vertebrae. The vertebrae vary in shape according to their location on the spine. Note some differences in shape, rotation, and function of the following sections:

Cartilaginous discs lie between the bodies of the vertebrae at the ventral (front) side of the vertebral column. Each disc is filled with a highly viscous fluid, which has a consistency resembling lava. The discs are spinal shock absorbers. Sufficient alignment and stretching contributes to the health of the discs.

The dorsal (back) side of each vertebra, except C1, C2, sacrum, and coccyx, has bony spinal processes that provide attachments for ligaments and muscles. The nerves from the spinal cord exit through intervertebral spaces along the dorsolateral aspect of the spine. The weave of paraspinal muscles up the back, contribute to postural support along with the discs.

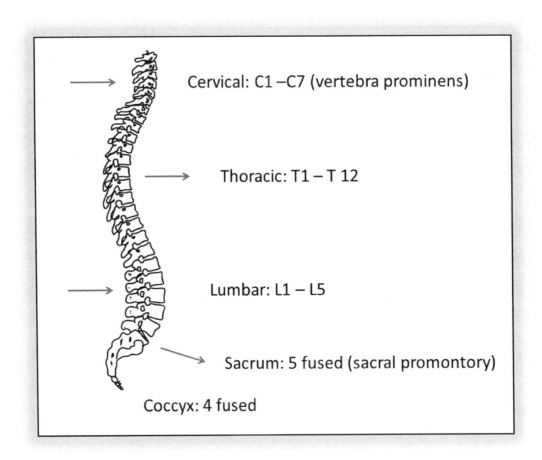

Cervical: C1 –C7 (vertebra prominens)

Thoracic: T1 – T 12

Lumbar: L1 – L5

Sacrum: 5 fused (sacral promontory)

Coccyx: 4 fused

Note the line of gravity through the body and where it falls.

Structure and Function

The lumbar spine supports the most weight. The vertebrae at the base of the spine are the largest, and the bony spinal processes inhibit twisting. The shape of the vertebral bodies and the processes support flexion and extension.

The thoracic spine supports the ribs. Synovial joints connect the ribs to the spinal processes in back. Because of the attachments of the ribs, the spinal extension of backbending is limited. The spine flexes forward, and straightens but does not go back. Because of the angle of the processes, twisting is possible, valuable for lengthening spinal muscles, and for the allied abdominal massage. The space between the discs diminishes during the twists and opens to refresh the joints after the twist. Because the space diminishes, alignment during the action of twisting is critical for the health of the spine.

The cervical spine has the greatest range of motion. The movements of flexion, extension and twisting support the facility of the cognitive senses. The top cervical vertebra is a pivot joint, where the weight of the head is given a wide and subtle range of movement.

Spinal misalignment can result from heredity factors, over-use, and trauma. Bad postural habits and gravity contribute to a deterioration of the structure of the spine.

Lordosis: exaggerated lumbar curve, "swayback"

Kyphosis: exaggerated thoracic curve, "dowager's hump"

Scoliosis: lateral bend and S-curve in spine; normally, goes left out of the base and curves to the right in the thoracic area.

Abdominal, Back and Neck Support

➢ *For this section, refer to anatomy resource materials and make any notes or sketches that you find pertinent. Particularly note the shapes and locations of the muscles, and consider poses that isolate and strengthen them.*

Abdominal Support

There are four main abdominal groups that, along with the ribs, enclose the internal organs, and provide support for our upright spine. Under-developed abdominal support and uneven abdominal support can cause structural problems and tension.

Rectus Abdominis - *'Rectus' lit. means 'straight'; known as the "six pack"*

Internal and External Obliques - *The main muscles of twisting*

Transversus Abdominis - *Lower ab support, wraps front to back; the "corset muscle"*

Ilio-Psoas - *The center of balance of torso into legs; can be activated by contracting longus colli in neck*

Muscles of the Back of the Torso

Trapezius - *Diamond shaped muscle of the upper back and neck; upper trapezius and lower trapezius are agonist/antagonist pairs*

Latissimus Dorsi - *A powerful pair of muscles that connects the fascial sheaths of the lower back across to the upper arms; the antagonists are the anterior deltoid and pectoralis major; antagonists are the anterior deltoid and pectoralis major*

Erector Spinae - *Multiple muscles of varying lengths that support ligaments of the spine*

Quadratus Lumborum - *Deepest back muscle, next to ilio-psoas on abdominal wall*

Into the Neck

Extensive layers of neck and shoulder muscle tissue ensure the rotation of the head. The muscles of the neck insert down the spine in the thoracic vertebrae.

➢ Find the following muscles in the neck area that connect head to shoulders.

Sterno-cleido-mastoid (SCM) - *Largest muscle for turning the head*

Splenius capitus - *Mediates action of muscles of thoracic spine into neck, also turning*

Levator Scapulae - *Connects occiput to scapulae*

Longus Colli - *Shortens throat, helps "tuck" hyoid bone into neck*

Into the Jaw and Temporomandibular Joint (TMJ)

This is a common area for muscular tension due to environmental stress. This tension can lead to headaches and jaw clenching and grinding. Unconscious grinding reduces tooth enamel and inflames the root nerves, which can create a need for root canals. In addition to the general relaxation of yoga that relieves jaw tension, opening the jaw wide in a pose such as "Lion" releases jaw clenching, as does releasing the tension of the eyes and the neck, particularly the SCM.

> ➤ Consider a few additional poses that might assist diminishing jaw tension:

The Bandhas

The bandhas are three holds or "locks" that support the upright spine and serve to enhance the vitality of the body. These traditional holds are engaged more powerfully during the breathing practices of *pranayama*. During asana practice, the discrete use of these holds aligns the spine.

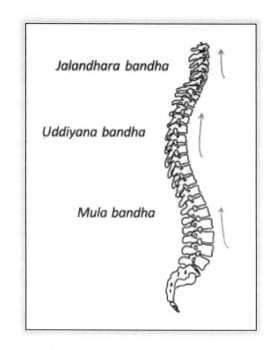

Lower spine: *Mula bandha*, the root hold

The muscular configuration of the pelvic floor and the pelvic diaphragm is the location of the *mula bandha*. The action of this bandha is not a clenching and squeezing of the perineum, but an engaging of the pelvic diaphragm to lift the floor. The paired action of the transversus abdominis and the gluteus medius assists the lift of the pelvic diaphragm. The lattisimus dorsi assists bracing the back.

60

Pelvic floor/diagram/perineum - an important note of distinction:

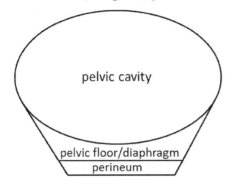

The pelvic floor, or pelvic diaphragm (the terms are used interchangeably), separates the pelvic cavity from the perineum. The pelvic diaphragm includes the levator ani and coccygeal muscles.

The perineum (often referred to as the urogenital triangle) is more superficial (closer to the skin) and includes the perinei muscles and fascia.

For further clarification, consider the diagram of the female pelvis (to the right). The view is looking down at the pelvic diaphragm from inside the torso. The urogenital triangle (perineum) is below this thin layer of muscle; we learn to distinguish these two areas and isolate the pelvic diaphragm for use with bandhas. (See additional discussion on the pelvis and these distinctions in chapter 4.)

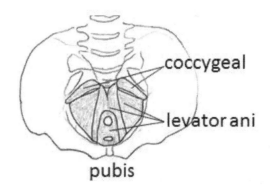

Middle spine: *Uddiyana bandha*, the upward-flying hold

The *uddiyana bandha* is the muscular action of higher abdominal muscles, the external obliques, to lift and lengthen the diaphragm, providing support for the middle spine. The paired extension of back muscles assists in creating length.

Upper spine: *Jalandhara bandha*, the throat hold

The *jalandhara bandha* aligns the chin closer to the throat, pulling the hyoid bone up and back, an action of the longus colli that supports the work of the ilio-psoas near the base of the spine. This uppermost bandha draws the spine to its full height. When the three bandhas are simultaneously activated in a pose such as *Mahamudra*, or great seal, they heighten awareness of the essence of asana practice: the combined muscular support of a healthy neutral spine and the vitality that comes with healthy alignment.

ASSIMILATION

Content

➤ List the anatomical names for the three divisions of the moving spine.

➤ What are the varying movements of the three parts of the spine? List the movements and the limitations due to the structure of the spine in each area.

➤ List the three bandhas in Sanskrit and English.

➤ Which abdominal muscle group does not support the internal organs?

– What is its function?

– How does its location contribute to its function?

➢ Where are the eight chakras located?

➢ List the koshas in Sanskrit and English.

➢ What are the eight limbs of Yoga?

Contemplation

Things to consider:

➢ Does our upright stance affect the shape of the spine?

➢ How might deterioration and misalignment of the spinal column affect other systems of the body?

➢ What is the virtue of these instruments?

- Body

- Five Cognitive Senses

- Five Active Senses

- Mind

- Ego

- Intellect

➢ When are you happiest? And least happy?

➢ Which one has the most power to prompt you to practice?

➢ Where do you notice yourself dwelling on your response to your environment? Is it where you are successful or where you fail to succeed?

➢ Have you had the experience of a friend's voice serving as a powerful witness? How did you feel?

➢ Has your relationship with your outer life and other people changed or shifted as a result of yoga? If so, how?

➢ Has your relationship with your inner world shifted? Thoughts or habits?

➢ When you close your eyes, where does your awareness travel?

➢ To which koshas do you feel most attached?

    – How do you experience them off the mat?

➢ When do you feel most subtle and what is your perception at that time?

Personal Practice

Spend time with seated poses. Feel the spine, breathe along the spine. Observe.

➤ Note any changes in your practice, day to day.

➤ Note any changes in yourself, day to day.

➤ Choose a pose and play with variations:
  - How does breath create variation?

  - How does breath increase awareness of the spine?

Salabhasana – Cobra

➤ Breathe out and in: what is the varying impact on belly and chest?

➤ What poses come before and after to prepare for cobra?

➤ Where do you find support? Vary the sphere of attention: Legs? Back? Gaze? Swallowing? Arm position? Belly/breath?

Choose a second pose for working with awareness of the spine:_____

- ➤ How does the pose create awareness of the spine? Consider your relationship to gravity.

- ➤ How does breathing in the pose impact awareness of the spine?

- ➤ How does the pose activate the energy of the spine?

Awareness of the back in practice:
- ➤ Can you feel deeper layers of the back muscle tissue? Can you name the muscle by feeling the tug of its tendons where the muscle attaches to the bones?

- ➤ What movement does that muscle assist?

- ➤ Can you trace the shape of the latissimus dorsi?

- ➤ Feel how contracting the upper trapezius relaxes the lower and vice versa. This one muscle contains an agonist-antagonist pair.

- ➤ Feel how the back supports breathing.

Awareness of the Core:

➢ Add some warm-up core strengtheners to your home practice. What are the results?

➢ How does swallowing assist the orientation of the posture of the spine?

Body Awareness:

➢ Locate the bandhas in mountain pose.

➢ What helps you relax the jaw? Does that softening help the muscles of the neck release?

Consider:

➢ How does the content of your study help you as an adult learner?

Poses

➤ Draw seated pose stick figures.
  (Axial extension, forward fold, twist, lateral extension)

➤ Add some arcs of movement – arms, spine, etc.

Wherever the fickle and unsteady mind wanders, he should subdue it
then and there and bring it back under the control of the self alone.
Bhagavad Gita 6/26

Chapter Three – Three Gunas

SS 4 -6 Purusha and the Three Gunas; Evolution and Involution
Begin assignment on the Three Gunas & Teaching Styles[1]

The story of the third chapter: the observer and the three qualities of nature that, due to their imbalance, create constant fluctuations in and out of form, in and out of activity, in and out of balance. The three qualities of light, movement, and stability are in an eternal dance of expression. Our inquiry into healthy movement moves to hips and shoulders, basic pairs of action and inhibition of action, how our body types can be categorized according to the gunas, and how every pose, every yoga session, and each person is an expression of the gunas.

Contents

---

[1] Complete information on written assignments is in the Appendix.

Energy dances while consciousness watches.
Devhuti

PHILOSOPHY

Samkhya Sutras 4 & 5: Purushah, The Three Attributes

Samkhya Sutra 4: Purushah

As we analyze energy and see that one field manifests in manifold fluctuations and forms from subtle to gross, the observer is effectively constellated. With the dawning awareness of an observing witness, we can seek more deeply to find the knower of the field of all modes and fluctuations: the real self. Consciousness and energy exist and project together from one ultimate source. Consciousness is *satchitananda* – the three qualities of existence, intelligence, and bliss; or truth, light and infinity. However we understand consciousness, what grows in our experience is that the mingling and identification of consciousness with energy leads to bondage. The separation of consciousness from the field of energy leads to freedom.

These two basic realms of seer and seen are variously described and expressed as:

Seer (*drastr*)	Seen (*drsya*)
Purusha	*Prakriti*
Observer	Observed
Eternal Stability	Endless Change
Knowledge	Compassion
Thought	Breath
Head	Heart
Being	Doing

The **observer** or consciousness is eternal, stable and unmoving.[2] The **observed** or energy is eternal, unstable, and moving. In yoga, the mind is trained to be one-pointed. Concentration leads to simplicity, clarity and happiness. The knowledge that energy moves and consciousness is stable is a guide by which we can anchor the self in consciousness. This allows us to respond more effectively to the constant fluctuations of nature. Patanjali explains that we end suffering by finding the distinction between seer and seen.

---

[2] An illustration of the power of the observing mind comes from physics in Heisenberg's "Uncertainty Principle." The influence of the observing mind impacts the behavior of subatomic particles. A photon has the behavior of both a particle and a wave, depending upon which behavior is sought by the observer.

> *Drastr-drsyayoh sanyogo heya-hetuh*   Y.S. II/17
> The cause of *heya*, what is to be ended (pain), is *sanyoga* – correlation between the *drastr*-seer and the *drsya*-the seeable.

Self and Soul

Is the self the same as the soul? According to this philosophy, the soul includes what is expansive in us as well as the more limited part of us that travels in life gathering impressions and personality. The self, the experience of the infinite, lies deep within us always watching, already free. The soul is made up of both our bondage and our freedom. The impressions of wrong knowledge cover the light of the self and the self is not recognized. We feel alien to ourselves in a state of bondage.

In the *brahma chakra* shines the light of the self. There our intelligence consciousness gives birth to the ego, the great gift. Through the ego we dance in the world, and through the ego we can seek back to the source. The waves of ego are called mind and give birth to "mine." All attachments to "me" and "mine" create darkness that covers the pure witness of the self. In the third verse of Patanjali's *sutras*, he tells us that when we are in yoga, the one who sees, the pure I-am, resides in its own essential nature.[3]

Undivided yet remaining as if divided in all beings,
This is known as the sustainer of beings their devourer and creator,
The light of lights beyond darkness, the knowledge seated in the hearts of all.
Bhagavad Gita 13/16-17

---

[3] *Tada drastuh svarupe 'vasthanam* Y.S. I/3. *Drasta* is a word for "the seer," the one who sees. The world of objects is called "the seen."

Samkhya Sutra 5: Three attributes

Developing awareness of the layers of projecting energy constellates our witness in pure consciousness. Consciousness is stable; energy moves. Kapil's analysis continues with the movement of the three *gunas*, the three attributes that constitute nature: light, movement and stability. The best way to feel them and to comprehend the difference between the ease of *sattoguna*, the activity of *rajoguna* and the heaviness and stability of *tamoguna* is to be still in meditation. Subtle distinctions are possible in quiet. If we endlessly engage in the swing between actions, *rajas*, to inert rest, *tamas*, we miss the balance point of *sattva*, which is the platform for our research into consciousness, the home of our real self.

The three qualities of energetic experience, light, movement, and stability are always present in differing combinations. Together they create the varieties of experience. In sitting practice, all three qualities are present. Vibrant health prepares us to sit. *Asana* releases the lethargy of *tamoguna* and calms the restlessness of *rajoguna* so the body is held with stability and ease, *sthira sukha*.[4] Then we look for a stable experience in the mind to use as a focal point. The movement of breath is helpful. The mind is restless; attending to the steady flow of breath soothes the mind. We create stability and calm, and then we can find reflection and ease. When the quality of *sattva* dominates, we approach causal energy where the light of consciousness shines through the highest center of intelligence in the *brahma chakra.* In Buddhism, the enlightened one is called a *boddhisattva*, one whose intelligence reflects the pure light consciousness and whose heart, freed of need, fills with compassion. In this balanced state, the three qualities are present in refined form as *sthiti, kriya,* and *prakash*, stability, subtle action, and luminous light, respectively.

When we turn inward, the place that welcomes us is an open place of tranquility and peace. At first, moving inward can seem like reducing ourselves because we are housed within the limitations of the body, but, within ourselves, we are truly large and whole. Our inner sanctuary is fullness, completeness, and satisfaction, a well from which we can drink before returning to work in the outer world of the senses. If we are satisfied within ourselves before we act, then we will not seek to complete ourselves through our actions. We can be of service to life. Our choices can be intelligent responses to circumstance, or what in this tradition is called duty. Duty refers to what needs to be done as opposed to the fancy mirages and dances of self-satisfaction. We simply do, and find peace in the doing. Our house will be in order. A quiet mind, choosing a safe harbor, rather than the storms of stimulation, can be focused, intentional, and loving. The quiet mind is a mountain summit from which we have calm perspective.

---

[4] Y.S. II/46: *sthira-sukham asanam.*

As teachers, this is important. How much more valuable our teaching of yoga will become when we feel complete within ourselves and can help our students find the same place. A teacher holds open the space for all students to grow within themselves. We have to hold that place open for ourselves first.

The distinction between seer and seen is not the normal distinction between subjective and objective. In this schema, body, senses, mind, ego, and intellect are "seen." They can all be known as instruments by the seer. The body is part of the gross world of objects where there is a predominance of *tamoguna*. The mind is energetic, moving – a predominance of *rajoguna*. In *sattoguna* we can hold all experience in reflection. Every possible experience is a dance of energy and consciousness. In meditation we seek to understand the *gunas* and when we are quiet, we can begin distinguishing between thought and awareness. Our thoughts also play among all three *gunas*: knowledge is *sattvic*, desire is *rajasic*, and dullness and sleepiness is *tamasic*. Consciousness sees all three—open as space through which thoughts move as wind. We gradually come to identify our selves with the seer – stable, peaceful, and fulfilled.

In practice, taming the restless mind can take many forms. The core idea is to create a one-pointed focus. Besides breath, the sound of a *mantra* is often used because it resonates through all energetic levels and draws us to one point. The mind delights in sound. *Mantras* are sounds whose intended purpose is to draw the mind inward toward the source of sound, not outward onto the senses. We draw the mind toward a resonant silence.

Our energetic instruments: causal to subtle to gross

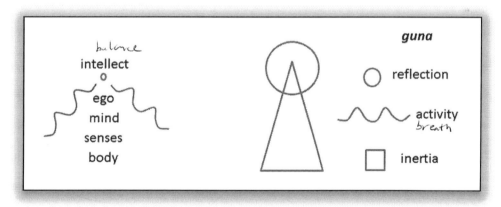

In the body, a natural focus for one-pointed concentration is between the eyes in the area of the pituitary and hypothalamus, a place where the nervous system and the endocrine system have an intimate and powerful relationship. When we find this focal point, our sitting practice is supported by a shift in our physiology.[5]

---

[5] How this occurs is currently beyond the understanding of science but not beyond our experience.

According to yoga, the point between the eyes and above the nose is the place of the ego, the I-amness. The ego creates the conscious container for our experience. Waves of thought are waves of ego, so if we withdraw into the center of the I-am between the eyes, the thought-waves naturally reduce and the activity of the mind calms. Withdrawing energy and awareness from the body, senses, and mind and into the area of the ego is involution of energy away from the gross and subtle, heading toward causal energy. It is calming and brings a one-pointed focus that is a platform for surrender to a higher intelligence and consciousness. Our awareness opens inward from this center of the ego to a larger experience of consciousness.

As the activity of the mind settles to stillness, awareness opens. After meditation, with the gunas in balance and awareness freed of mental clamoring, we return to the movements of the gunas. Then we learn to guide our experience with the light of consciousness. In the light of sattoguna, our actions take place. Wisdom and compassion are possible.

Samkhya Sutra 6: Evolution and Involution

Through evolution, nature develops all the means of knowing and acting. Once they are developed in human life, then practice is possible. Practice is involution, moving back toward the source. It is not energy that seeks its source; the soul as consciousness, uses energy as a means of seeking the source. This seeking is called the practice of yoga, as opposed to seeking experience, called *bhoga.* Our seeking is based on our knowledge. The five sources of knowledge are given after suffering is explained more fully. Suffering or knowledge—both Kapil and Patanjali[6] present our choices.

On a cosmic level, there is no discussion of the purpose of life, only that it exists, it expresses, it resolves and it eternally continues. We can suffer or we can be free.

---

[6] "The seen has the characteristics of luminous light, activity, and stability. It is embodied in the elements and sense organs and exists for the dual purpose of experience and emancipation." Y.S II/18

METHOD

Teaching Method and the Three Gunas

Once we understand the *gunas*, the constant movement of nature, and have experienced the freedom and peace of balance and quiet, our teaching has a basis. We can now use the movement of the *gunas* to serve our teaching and help others learn how to feel them and work with them. This is the essence of Sāmkhya philosophy and why it is placed as the basis of yoga. All yoga practices use energy in service of consciousness. Our daily responsibilities are more often ruled by the demands of nature than guided by the light of consciousness. When we reverse this, we create an enormous shift from bondage to liberation. Patanjali has given this knowledge in *Yoga Sutras* II/18: "The seen has the characteristics of luminous light, activity, and stability. It is embodied in the elements and sense organs and exists for the dual purpose of experience and emancipation." *Bhoga* means experience through the senses where we gather information and learn or we are compelled by a desire for fulfillment. Yoga means emancipation, freedom from craving – the seer stands alone. We continue to live among the *gunas*, but we satisfy our hunger not our greed.

> *Prakaasha-kriya-sthito-silam bhutendriyaatmakam bbhogaapavargaartham drshyam*
> Y. S. II/18
>
> | | |
> |---|---|
> | *Prakasha* | brightness, intelligence, *sattoguna* |
> | *Kriya* | activity, *rajoguna* |
> | *Sthito* | inertia, *tamoguna* |
> | *Silam* | characteristic |
> | *Bhuta* | elements |
> | *Indriya* | sense organs |
> | *Atmakam* | having the nature of, embodied by |
> | *Bhoga* | experience |
> | *Apavarga* | emancipation |
> | *Artham* | purpose |
> | *Drshyam* | what is to be seen, the seeable |

The three *gunas* organize our approach as teachers. The qualities shift and play in our students, our moods, the time of year, the practices we share, in the art of teaching a pose, and in the arc of a class. We can start by finding the *gunas* in three broad categories: knowledge, movement, containment in the body.

Knowledge is Sattvic:
Our knowledge base includes philosophy, anatomy, technique, and method. The more precise our knowledge, the more precise is our teaching.

Skill in teaching is dependent upon our knowledge and skill in solving problems. If a difficulty arises in class, it is best addressed efficiently and compassionately and then followed up with after the session. Our skill in making choices is a long process. Some say it takes ten years to make a yoga teacher. Teaching skills require both a knowledge base and many hours of teaching and personal practice.

Movement is Rajasic:
The poses are a vocabulary of movements that reach into the human experience beyond the conscious mind, through all the sheaths of our energetic experience and memory.

Containment is Tamasic:
Yoga works through the nervous system, the sensory-motor system, autonomic functions, and the regulations of the lower brain. All systems of the body are impacted: cardio-respiratory, digestive, immune, endocrine and musculoskeletal. The gross movements assist the homeostasis of the body, and impact interrelationship among the other systems. The systems of the body constitute one exquisite network of communication and feedback that is tuned by our practice.[7]

We bring to our teaching the knowledge of the body, our experience of living in a human body, the inspection of what works for us in our own practice, an understanding of a class setting, the challenges of teaching to a group, and skill in presentation.

The first step in teaching is observing the class.
Method is the application of knowledge by virtue of our speech into the setting and the bodies in front of us. The setting includes the space, the needs of the students and the number of people present. Experienced teachers learn to adjust their approach according to the fluctuations of each teaching situation.

The primary sattvic intervention is to observe the class:
- The range of motion of the students.
- The needs of the group, both explicit and implicit.

  An explicit need might be a brief rest at the onset of class before moving.
  An implicit need might be to let go of the demands of the ego.

Rajasic intervention is warming up the tissues and opening body awareness:
- Instruct awareness of breath.
- Instruct movement with the breath.

These two actions retain the value of sattva while initiating movement.

---

[7] A relatively new branch of research into interdependence of the various systems of the body is called psychoneuroimmunoendocrinology (PNIE).

Tamasic considerations lie in the health of the body:
- The body seeks homeostasis.
- The body contains experience.

The body seems to feel better when it moves, but truly it is indifferent. The body does not care if it is sick, or stiff, or even if it dies. The mind cares. The mind is not indifferent. The mind and ego have clear preferences in the form of likes and dislikes. Wisdom likes the whole process; it enjoys learning and discerning.

The Three Gunas in the Poses: Alignment

When we teach a pose, the three gunas can guide our instruction. Begin instruction with the gross form: how the ground and base support the pose. Then there is action within the form: highlighting muscles that assist alignment and bringing out the virtue of the posture. The virtue becomes the sattvic aspect—what is enlivened, known and learned through the posture.

Every pose can be taught with a foundation in the gunas:

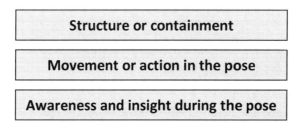

Structure or containment

Movement or action in the pose

Awareness and insight during the pose

Each pose stands alone and within a sequence. In sequence, the previous pose carries an impression or memory in the mind and the body which informs the next pose. One pose following another can also teach alignment by activating muscles that are then used or released in the next. Careful sequencing creates movement in the light of awareness—a sattvic intention.

The Three Gunas in the Arc of the Class: Sequencing

Now consider the arc of a class and how knowledge of the gunas is embedded within it. In the beginning of a session, we typically come to practice with a predominance of either lethargy or distraction. The opening should address the need for releasing fatigue and quieting distraction. There are many ways to do this, and a class will have shifting dynamics with the gunas depending on the time of day, the season and general activity levels. Winter is a dormant season; spring is energetic. In the morning we are stiff from sleep but we have more energy. At the end of the day the body is more flexible but we are tired from the day's activities.

Brahmana and Langhana:
Once the session is underway, we have choices to heat and cool the body called brahmana and langhana. Naturally these two are related with rajoguna and tamoguna. Brahmana means inspiring and expanding. Langhana is cooling and softening. Energetic work and releasing work are both done with awareness, which makes them sattvic. We do not overly push the body or cave into lethargy. Fatigue, heaviness and heedlessness need to be lifted with ragoguna before practice can become sattvic.

At the end of the session, we cultivate awareness along with stillness in the motor system and create a balance between the best of wakefulness and the best of sleep. The two combined establish a sattvic state in our nervous system that allows us to be restfully alert and to carry on the task of life with more awareness and less dominance of rajoguna and tamoguna.

He who knows the truth about the two roles of the gunas, experience and liberation, while acting knows that the gunas move among the gunas and is not attached.
Bhagavad Gita 3/28

The Three Gunas in our Bodies, the Doshas

The goal of our hatha yoga practice is to find balance, but our starting points differ. These differences can be understood through the knowledge of the doshas that comes from Ajurveda. Varying body types and correlated inclinations are due to qualities of the gunas that are categorized into these basic doshas. The goal of Ajurvedic medicine is to balance the doshas. In this system, the grossest, tamoguna, is related with earth and water, the more subtle rajoguna is related with the movement of fire and heat, and the subtlest, sattoguna, with air. From heaviest to lightest, the doshas are kapha, pitta and vata, earth/water, fire, and air. Traditionally, the doshas have been correlated with a diagnostic technique basing all diseases on imbalances of phlegm, bile, and wind.

Individuals can adjust their practices to accommodate the needs of their dohsas. For instance, a kapha type benefits from a vigorous, heated practice. A vata type would be overwhelmed by such a practice and would need a gentler practice. A pitta type might be drawn to a heated practice but this might not encourage the balance in the nervous system that would come with a combination of heating and cooling.

Again our starting point as teachers is to become familiar with our own dosha and how to meet our own needs. Then we can become more sensitive to the varying needs of others and encourage a valuable practice. Each group has a variety of doshas. If we vary our focus and offer a variety of classes and styles, we can educate people to help themselves.

	VATA	PITTA	KAPHA
Physical build	light	medium	sturdy
Weight	low weight gain	moderate	high weight gain
Frame	delicate, thin	moderate	large-boned
Joints	strain easily	normal	well-formed, lubricated
Musculature	slight	medium & firm	thick
Hips & shoulders	narrow	medium	broad
Nails	brittle	oval & pink	square, large, pale
Balanced mental state	creative	organized	satisfied
Imbalanced mental state	scattered, fearful	angry, possessive	rarely upset, content
Hatha practice needs	grounding	cooling	heating

The Three Gunas and Homeostasis

Stress and Homeostasis

When we engage in a yoga practice we are setting up conditions in the body to facilitate healing. Neither we as teachers, nor any members of the medical profession, have the capacity or ability to heal a body. It is set up to heal itself, and under certain conditions, healing is more efficient. Homeostasis, a state of physiological equilibrium produced by a balance of functions and of chemical composition within an organism, assists healing. The body seeks homeostasis. The massaging effect of yoga, the alignment and stretch of connective tissue, the stimulation of all the systems of the body assist a reach toward a flexible state where fluctuations in response to the environment are available. When the system continually reacts to a stressful environment, it becomes rigid. Backing the systems of the body off the edge of stress, as it were, assists our individual organism to maintain itself and its interdependent systems at the highest levels of functioning.

Perception shifts though yoga practice. Perception of life as a challenge rather than a threat, the ability to pause before responding, the ability to evaluate the environment in healthier ways all contribute to stress hardiness. The acceptance of the unacceptable is the great teaching of equanimity. The value of deep relaxation during the practice of yoga is that we gain time for the response to threat to completely leave the nervous system. The body seeks a deep state of balance in that time.

The relationship between a healthy body, perception, and emotions is currently the basis of scientific research.[8] Research is being done under the auspices of the National Institute of Health (NIH). [9]

---

[8] *Molecules of Emotion*, Candice Pert, Ph.D.
[9] In the 1990's funding was increased the same year the NIH accepted acupuncture as a reasonable and rational medical treatment. Their acceptance was based on the efficacy of acupuncture as a pain treatment.

Historically, Eastern systems of medicine such as Ajurveda, acupuncture, and yoga have not divorced treatment of the mind and emotions from the body. In the West, treatment of mind and body are traditionally integrated only in the field of psychiatry. Traditional Eastern Medicine accepts the intimate correlation of mind, emotions and the body, and the impact on both by the external environment. Health is not freedom from disease but a state of optimal functioning of both mind and body.

The Goldilocks Principle: Exaggeration, Depletion and Just Right.
Given a long, sunny morning to oneself for yoga practice, rambling about the house of the body, you might stumble on the Goldilocks principle. As you rock lazily in and out of poses, stand to challenge yourself and sink back to the earth to release tension, you are living the Goldilocks principle. You try something and find it too much. You try something else and find it too little. You find something just right and stay there. Then you begin again. You are seeking a balance between too much and too little.

In the musculoskeletal system, as a tight muscle gets tighter it threatens to have a decreased blood flow and cramping. Stretching increases blood flow in the capillaries feeding the muscle tissue and reducing the threat of cramping. A muscle with too little muscle tone is also lacking circulation as muscular action aids the vascular system. If muscles are slack, a sudden movement can damage muscle and connective tissue. Joints are another example – when muscles are too tight, joints have restricted range of motion, and when too loose, there is hypermobility and instability. Optimum functioning is somewhere between too tight and too slack. Yoga can be thought of as the constant application of the Goldilocks principle throughout the systems of the body as we attend to sensations, motor response, perception and emotions.

The central nervous system consists of the brain and spinal cord (see Diagram of the Nervous System on next page). The autonomic nervous system is a motor system independent of somatic movement. It consists of two major divisions, the sympathetic and parasympathetic, which work together to regulate our internal milieu. Some examples are control of heart rate, digestive movement, respiration, thirst and hunger. During heightened arousal, the sympathetic division is oriented to attend to the external environment. The parasympathetic division of the autonomic nervous system is responsible for renewal. This has been coined "the relaxation response."[10] In deep relaxation, we sustain parasympathetic dominance for a longer period of time in order to restore optimum homeostasis.

Hans Seyle[11] has proposed three stages of the stress response. The first is the alarm reaction where mobilization includes accelerated heart rate and respiration. The second phase is called the stage of resistance where the body adapts to stressors and inhibits reactions that are not directly needed to deal with the stressors, thus maximizing the

---

[10] *The Relaxation Response*, Herbert Benson,
[11] *The Stress of Life*, Hans Seyle, 1956.

efficiency of the response. In the third phase, if adaptation is not adequate and the stressors persist at an intense level, the body reaches a stage of exhaustion.

Within Yoga philosophy, the three qualities of nature describe the three stages of arousal, adaptation, and fatigue. The correlation with the three gunas is rajas, sattva, and tamas, respectively. The state of sattva, which is translated variously as balance or ease, a state that brings a sense of renewal to the practitioners of yoga, also describes the state of parasympathetic dominance. Within the cultivation of a deep state of renewal through yoga practice, adaptation to stress is enhanced.

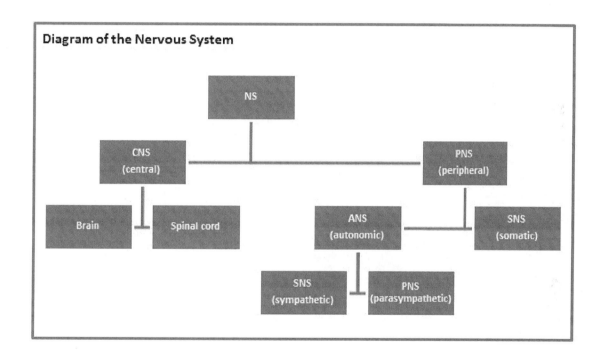

TECHNIQUE

Yoga Therapy

The Doshas
Of the three doshas of kapha, pitta and vata, we tend to have a body type and personality related with two primary doshas; therefore, we are able to make only the simplest of observations regarding the three types. Pitta characteristics will incline people toward vigorous yoga when they might, instead, be better balanced with a more gentle and restorative practice. Vata types will have a body that appears able to push, but forcing this type can lead to a pitta imbalance. A kapha body, which may be sturdier or rounder, benefits the most from a vigorous practice.

Principles
- ✓ Observe the range of motion. Instruct simple poses that allow you to observe the spectrum of the class, e.g. arms over the head, sitting on heels.

- ✓ Observe the state of the gunas. Are the students restless or lethargic?

- ✓ If restless, get them moving before static poses and breathing with the movement.

- ✓ If lethargic, breathe with static poses to restore energy then get them moving.

- ✓ Observe alignment issues. Work with the most obvious problems first and with the weakest member. The whole group will benefit and everyone can participate. Look for rounded shoulders, jutting chins, alignment in the feet etc. Allow individuals to seek their own body awareness via careful instructions before assisting with touch. Then, when you assist, guide the whole group, one by one, in one pose.

- ✓ Instruct pieces of the pose before putting them together, e.g. instruct the arms separately, then the base, then together.

- ✓ Give modifications gradually, e.g. each time you return to child's pose, give an additional modification. Then ask them to choose their own modification, e.g. extended arms, forehead on forearms, or hands by feet.

- ✓ Choose a sequence that leads to a pose so that the body is ready for all aspects of the form, e.g. do many simple twists and lunges before a lunging twist.

Alignment is agreement

Agreement implies that "a thing can be known," which is a definition of sattva. Rajas, which is passionate, and tamas, which is heedless, do not breed agreement. Passion blinds perception; lethargy blurs perception. Seeking healthy alignment is a process of seeking agreement with ourselves.

Hatha yoga reduces the power of pre-existing conditions and replaces them with what is intrinsically authentic. When we return to the authentic, there is inherent agreement. With authenticity, our feeling of ease increases and our nervous system relaxes. Another word for the ease of sattva is *sukha*. *Sukha* is the opposite of *dukha*, or pain. Pain in life comes from the bondages of attachment and craving that leads to further enmeshment and identification with the material world. We favor asana that creates *sukha*, not *dukha*. Patanjali defines asana as *stira sukha*—stable ease. This is a sattvic state that is non-fluctuating. Alignment helps us find and sustain stable ease.

The observing self is cultivated in a sattvic practice. Freedom lies within the seer, the observer. With a sustained practice, a sense of self develops that is based on continuity of consciousness, rather than the outcome of our actions that are either successes or failures. Our relationship with self is improved. Self-identity becomes based on evolution of consciousness. Continuity of this memory leads to a dynamic sense of self, independent of circumstances.

Instructions based on the Three Gunas

The three gunas are inextricably within every moment and every movement of nature, and within every expression and impulse of energy. How we see and feel the gunas depends on how we are looking for them.

Tamas: The ground is the shape of the pose, where to place the hands and feet—how to construct the base for the action of the pose.

Rajas: The action of a pose moves from distal, what is far → to proximal, what is near. We open our instruction with how to move hands and feet to create a pose, and then for the action within a posture, we give instructions closer to the core and center, including the breath, the spine and abdominal support. Instructions of action within the posture then shift to include how support near the center radiates to the periphery. We move with direction. Isometric pushing or pulling within the base and core create the aligned action of the pose. Learning the appropriate action within each posture takes time and patience.

Sattva: What can be known is not confined to the posture itself. Since every person is working within all of their energetic sheaths, thoughts can range to any level of experience. The range of the koshas goes from gross to subtle to causal. The instruction regarding base and movement can lead to a sattvic state of reflection that is both universal and personal. Sattva is a balance of tamas and rajas. So when the base and the action are well balanced the sattvic quality of reflection naturally opens.

As you learn to instruct postures, discrete language surrounding base and action are necessary for an uncluttered experience. Gradually add variations to help the students stay focused. Sattvic elements reveal themselves—some can be highlighted with verbal instruction, some will come within silence.

Asanas and Their Benefits:[12] Annamayakosha

Below are listed four categories of poses and their benefits on the physical body, the level of tamoguna. Also included are the heating and cooling aspects of brahmana and langhana so you can begin to see how physiological balance is created through the postures.

Forward Folds - Annamayakosha

→ Lengthen spine making it supple and elastic.
→ Invigorate nervous system.
→ Complete stretch to posterior body, relieving compression of spine and sciatica.
→ More extended stretch with relaxed neck and head.
→ Stretch and strengthen hamstrings.
→ Increase blood supply to brain, while lowering blood pressure via baroreceptors in carotid artery and aorta.
→ Powerful massage to internal organs, stimulating and toning digestive system, relieving indigestion and constipation.
→ Increase peristalsis and regulate pancreatic function.
→ Counteract obesity and enlargement of spleen and liver.

Langhana is emphasized, although some balance with brahmana, encouraging vital energy necessary for meditation.

Twists - Annamayakosha

→ Tone the roots of the spinal nerves and sympathetic nervous system, thereby reducing spine, hip and groin problems.
→ Increase the synovial fluid of the joints for general health and reduction of the symptoms of arthritis.
→ Squeeze, massage, and stimulate abdominal organs and muscles releasing toxins and bringing fresh blood supply.
→ Balance hormones.

Balances brahmana and langhana.

---

[12] Derived from material compiled by Marianne Rieske. References: *Yoga: Mind and Body*, Shivananda Yoga Vedanta Center, DK Publishing, *Yoga Teacher's Toolbox*, Joseph and Lilian LePage.

Lateral Bends - Annamayakosha

→ Open ribs and intercostals muscles, creating space for breath, circulation of blood and lymph.
→ Ankles, legs, hips and arms sustain healthy range of motion.
→ Squeeze, massage and stimulate internal organs, bringing fresh blood supply, releasing toxins and wastes, and stimulating immune function.
→ Tone spinal nerves and massages organs of elimination.
→ Improve appetite by assisting digestion.
→ Reduce low back pain.

Langhana is emphasized with some brahmana.

Hip Range of Motion - Annamayakosha

→ Increase circulation and flexibility in hips, legs, knees, and groin.
→ Offer pelvic stabilization and strengthening to low back while aligning and lengthening spine.
→ Alleviate low back pain and sciatica.
→ Massage and purify abdominal organs aiding digestion/elimination problems.
→ Massage reproductive organs and assist menstruation.
→ Stimulate immune function in lymph nodes in groin.

Most are langhana with some balancing with brahmana.

Sequencing: Yoga for Meditation

This is a series of seated and supine poses intended to balance the gunas, moving from tamas to rajas to sattva. Also, the series opens areas of the body that may be tense, so that turning the mind inward in a seated pose is stable and easy.

Breathing standing:
Arms wide   Rotate thumbs and follow with breath and spine

Lunge breath: Short lunge stance

neutral   inhale wide   exhale forward (5-10x)   lengthen forward   neutral

1 – flying bird forward fold (ff)

start with length…   inhale, lengthen spine…   exhale ff & hang…   inhale up…

2 – half-moon (shoulders)

exhale one hand forward…   inhale back…   rotate up…   exhale opposite shoulder down

3 – *counterpose*
    squat

4 – wall hang
    (shoulders & hips)

                start   step back   *breathe…*

Moving to floor – press low back down first as you go

1 – look at toes and hold

2 – head lifts with hands...   heavy head   twist gently

Breathing with spine:

neutral   inhale   exhale (scoop)   inhale   exhale   neutral

1 – knee to chest pose

2 – spinal twist

3 – *counterpose*... knee circles and spinal wobbles (head and knees opposite way)

Sitting: hip openers
1 – sit on heels   sit to left of ankles   open bottom leg   bow to the left

 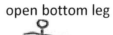 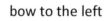

2 – lengthen up   go on left elbow   hand on right hip   breathe and move

3 – lean to left and straighten back leg...
    bring it to the front and cross knee

4 – then forward fold

5 – straighten legs in front… "windshield wiper" the feet, repeat left

Back on elbows:

1 – slouch   and lift carefully, back with head at end

Rest on back…

Pranayama:

sitting inhale (hold 7 counts)   exhale closing one nostril   refreshing breath

repeat 3x each side

sit

What lies behind us and what lies before us are tiny matters
as compared with what lies within us.
Oliver Wendell Holmes

PRACTICUM

Keep it Simple: What Makes a Good Yoga Class?

Basics for a good class:
1. Environment
2. Progressive series of postures
3. Consistent rhythm
4. Clear, concise cues
5. Voice tone and projection
6. Breath
7. Authenticity

What makes it great?
1. Connections
   a. Eye contact
   b. Help students use their props
   c. Physical assists
   d. Recognition of effort and growth in your students
2. Enlightenment
   a. Teaching from the heart
   b. Inspiration
   c. Application to daily life
3. Authenticity

How to go from good to great:
1. Be present
2. Know your sequence and cues so well that you can refocus your energy on seeing and connecting with your students, instead of remembering what pose comes next
3. Get to know your students
4. Give your students something to take with them
5. Trust the practice. It can stand on its own. You don't need to do anything fancy.
6. Do the work
   a. 75% of your teaching skills comes from your own, personal practice
   b. Make it to your mat.
   c. Keep up a regular meditation practice
7. Teach what you love.
   a. Why do you love yoga? Teach that, and you will be great.

Bless the shoulders
For they are a strength and a shelter.

Bless the hips
For they are cunning beyond all other machinery.
Mary Oliver

ANATOMY

Alignment of Hips and Shoulders

The purpose of healthy alignment is to lessen the stress on the joints while in the postures. We amplify what can move well and reduce the risk of strain in weaker areas. For example, greater rotation of the hips when the legs are folded and externally rotated will reduce the strain on the knee.

Ligaments stabilize the joints and allow mobility. Because ligaments have less blood flow, which means slow repair when injured, we need to refine our understanding of their function and stay aware of the joint positions. Ligaments are thicker in the hips and thinner in the shoulders. In the hips, the ligaments help stabilize the bones. In the shoulders, the muscles stabilize the bones. In the shoulders, primary stabilization lies in the rotator cuff and the secondary stabilization is the tricep/bicep pair.

Understanding agonist/antagonist pairs helps to stabilize movement. By definition, when the agonist contracts, the antagonist is inhibited. However, for the purpose of creating a stable posture, we often engage the lengthened antagonist in eccentric contraction. The paired action strengthens the posture. (See figure below.)

Another way that we support balanced action is by reversing the normal contraction of a muscle. In an open chain contraction, we might we fold our arm to lift a heavy object. The center of the body supports movement farther from the center. Using open chain contractions supports balance and awareness of the body in space. Using the forearms to support the weight on the body in an inversion is a closed chain contraction—the reverse. In a closed chain contraction we become aware of the use of our core.

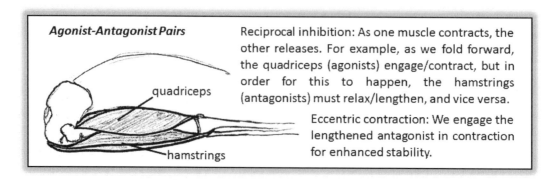

Agonist-Antagonist Pairs

quadriceps

hamstrings

Reciprocal inhibition: As one muscle contracts, the other releases. For example, as we fold forward, the quadriceps (agonists) engage/contract, but in order for this to happen, the hamstrings (antagonists) must relax/lengthen, and vice versa.

Eccentric contraction: We engage the lengthened antagonist in contraction for enhanced stability.

Anatomy of the Pelvic Girdle (Legs)

Develop an understanding of the pelvic area by noting there are three major bones of the pelvis. The sacrum of the spine is included in the pelvic girdle.

The joints between the pelvis and the sacrum are the sacro-iliac joints.

Locate the perineum or urogenital triangle and understand its basic shape.

Find the pelvic diaphragm, shaped like an inverted bell, that contracts to lift the pelvic floor.

Find the connective tissue called the peritoneum, which holds the inner organs above the bladder and sexual organs.

Concerns for Yoga Teachers

The base of the spine lies in the pelvic area between the ilia (singular, ilium). The fused vertebral area called the sacrum rests directly between these two wide pelvic bones. The spine and hips are thus connected at the sacro-iliac joint, which is a problematic area during yoga practice. If this joint is over-stretched, tendons are lengthened (bone to muscle), ligaments between the bones are lengthened and the area becomes unstable, leading to further injury.

Another area of concern in the hips and lower back is the sciatic nerve. Its point of origin is near lumbar vertebrae 4 & 5 and it courses under a rotator muscle behind the iliac crest called the piriformis. The sciatic nerve has a diameter approximate to that of the middle finger. If it is impinged upon, it remains inflamed for about a month. During that time, avoiding re-inflammation is critical. With sciatic pain, the hip and entire leg are subject to numbing and/or pain. To alleviate the condition, time and patience are required, and yoga can help. Poses that continue to inflame the area should be discontinued. This proves difficult because a forward bend is the intuitive response to back pain and is the worst choice for relief from sciatica, since it aggravates the nerve. Mild backbends and axial extensions are helpful.

Hips and Legs

Locate the three major bones of the legs: the femur, the tibia and fibula. Note how the femur inserts into a pivot joint within acetabulum. This joint is deeper than the similar shoulder pivot joint, and protected by ligaments.

Internal and external rotation of the hip is accomplished by muscles that also assist with forward motion. They are large muscles -- the gluteus maximus and medius. A deeper layer of finer external rotator muscles behind the pelvic girdle includes the piriformis. As mentioned above, tension in the piriformis is one source of the condition of sciatica. The other main contributing factor to sciatic pain is a spinal injury at L4/L5 or L5/sacrum.

Abduction, that is moving away from the midline, is also an action of the gluteus muscles. Adduction, moving back toward the midline involves large muscles on the inner thigh. The adductor group

| Note to help remember: |
| Abduction, absent, away |
| Adduction, addition, towards |

protects the legs and can be a viable area of resistance in yoga poses. The sartorius is a long thin muscle that assists bending and abduction of the knee. The iliotibial band is a long band of connective tissue on the lateral side of the leg that stabilizes the femur. One of the gluteus muscle group, the tensor fascia latae, attaches directly to the iliotibial band, helps extend the knee and assists with inward rotation. All these are landmark areas for posture instruction.

Agonist antagonist pairs in the Hips and Legs:

Location	Agonist	Action	Antagonists
Inner hip	Iliopsoas	Folds leg	Gluteus maximus & hamstrings
Outer hip	Glut. max.	Extends leg	Iliopsoas & rectus femoris
Under outer hip	Glut. medius	Lifts/opens leg	Adductors
Femur to hip	Pectineus	Closes leg	Gluteus medius
Inside thigh	Add. magnus	Closes leg	Gluteus medius
Under glut. max.	Piriformis	Ext. rotation	Adductors & gluteus medius
Top thigh	Quads	Folds hip	Hamstrings & gastrocnemius
Top thigh	Quads	Extends knee	Sartorius & gracilis
Back thigh	Hamstrings	Folds knee	Quads & iliopsoas
Back thigh	Hamstrings	Extends hip	Quads & iliopsoas

Refer to anatomy resources for further study.

Knees

The knee is a vivid example of a joint capsule. The layers of ligaments are part of the joint capsule. The unusual padding of the meniscus, inside the joint between the two ends of cartilage, protects the knee during lateral rotation. Note the attachments of the muscles of the thigh below the knee to assist bending the knee. The rectus femoris (the central muscle of the quadriceps) attaches behind the patella to help straighten the leg.

The knees fold to help us move and at the same time are powerful shock absorbers. Note the size and shape of the knee joint in relation to the size of the bones of the leg to see how the structure of the knee supports this function.

The knee is vulnerable to rotation. Many yoga poses externally rotate the bent leg. We need to include poses that stabilize the knee and observe its alignment while rotated so that we do not weaken its structure during practice.

Feet and Ankles

The foot and ankle have multiple bones and three arches that assist forward motion, dorsiflexion and plantarflexion, and provide the versatility of movements called pronation and supination, inversion and eversion. The heel bears the weight of the body. The arch into the toes is more critical for movement. Standing poses are based in the three major arches of the feet, medial and lateral arches and the transverse arch.

Anatomy of the Shoulder Girdle (Arms)

The first step in understanding the value of yoga for the shoulders and arms is to gain an accurate body map of the area. Find the collar bones, noting their synovial joints at the sternum are the only juncture of the shoulder girdle to the axial skeleton. The collarbone attaches to a finger of bone that comes off the top of the scapula, the acromion. The humerus bone of the upper arm, attaches in a shallow pivot joint on the side of the scapula.

Movement of the Scapulae

The scapulae move up and down, in and out, and upward with rotation.

	Direction:	Term:	Muscle group(s) involved:
	Up	Elevation	Upper trapezius, levator scapulae
	Down	Depression	Lower trapezius
	In	Retraction (adduction)	Trapezius, rhomboids
	Out	Protraction (abduction)	Serratus anterior
	Up w/ rotation	Upward rotation	Upper trapezius, serratus anterior
	Medial	Internal rotation (hands face back)	Subscapularis

	Lateral	External rotation (hands face front)	Supraspinatus, infraspinatus, teres minor

(More on shoulders and arm movement in Chapter 6 - Arm Balances)

The lateral rotation of the arm that we favor in many yoga postures protects the bursa in the shoulder. A bursa is a synovial sac, a padding that protects the joint from the friction of movement. Without lateral rotation during upward rotation of the arm, the humerus presses against the acromial area and wears on the bursa. With lateral rotation, there is little compression and greater movement in the shoulder.

The biceps flex the elbows. The triceps extend the elbow. In addition, strong movers of the shoulders and arms are the pectoralis major and minor and the deltoids. Adding strength to length is a goal of yoga postures so that the strong muscles do not retain a short muscle memory that would inhibit full range of motion. Shortened muscles compress joints, and create long-term wear and tear.

The forearm has two bones that are either parallel or crossed, the radius and ulna. With the arms outstretched and the hands supinated, these bones are parallel. When we turn just the hands down in pronation, holding the upper arms steady, the radius crosses the ulna. This is a stable position for downward facing dog and arm balance poses.

Agonist Antagonist Pairs in the Shoulders and Arms:

Location	Agonist	Action	Antagonists
Top of chest	Pec. major	Lifts	Biceps & external rotators
Between shoulder blades	Rhomboids	Pulls shoulders back	Serratus anterior, lower traps & pec. major
Side ribs	Serratus anterior	Flattens scapulae	Rhomboids (paired in triangle)
Top of shoulders	Deltoids	Lifts arms	Lattisimus dorsi, pec. major & triceps
Front of arm	Biceps	Folds elbow	Triceps

Refer to anatomy resources for further study.

Wrist and Hand
The hand has 25 joints and 58 movements. The carpel bones in the wrist have gliding joints between them. The thumb is a saddle joint. There is a body image in the brain of sensory input from touch and proprioception. This body map, the "homunculus," has large hands and lips compared to the rest of the body.

ASSIMILATION

Content

➢ What are the two fundamental principles of one supreme power? Describe them in a few different ways.

➢ Describe the three gunas.

➢ What are the two words for heating and cooling in Sanskrit?

➢ How do these terms correlate with the movement of the spine and breathing during hatha practice?

➢ What is mula bandha? Why do we use it?

Contemplation

➢ How do you see the gunas at work during a hatha yoga practice?

➢ The three gunas are present in every moment as ideas, movement and containment. Can you feel how you carry these three areas simultaneously in the different instruments of the body?

➢ As a teacher, which guna might you favor?

➢ When we climb stairs what main muscle contracts in the thigh to lift the bent leg?

➢ Is a synergist of that lift the iliopsoas?

Personal Practice

➢ When do you feel most yourself?

➢ How does your practice support that experience?

➢ How does your practice reflect your doshas?

➢ What are a few ways to address fatigue during your hatha sessions?

➢ Can you deepen the experience of sattva during relaxation?

Poses

➢ Draw stabilizing poses.

➢ Draw a series of 12 poses that includes all categories introduced thus far (warm-ups, axial extension, forward folds, twists, lateral extension, hip ROM and stabilizing).

To him who sees Me in every self and sees every self in Me.
I am not lost to him and he is not lost to Me.
Bhagavad Gita 6/30

Chapter Four – Observer and observed

SS 4 -6 Purusha and the Three Gunas; Evolution and Involution
Written assignment due on the Three Gunas & Teaching Styles

The story of the fourth chapter: Standing poses open breath and circulation and help us to observe more globally. In these poses, we come to understand how the legs support the spine and the breath, and the arms support the breath and the spine. The movements of the legs and hips profit from hip range of motion exercises prior to standing and the practice of standing poses will stabilize a healthy hip ROM. Standing poses require careful counterposes, and lead to a vibrant deep relaxation.

Contents

Normally our consciousness serves energy.
In practice, energy serves consciousness.
devhuti

PHILOSOPHY

Revisit Samkhya Sutras 4 – 6

These few sutras are the heart of the Samkhya sutras and the essence of the Yoga method. We can find the observer of all energy and then note how the observer is akin to space, an open place of observation that takes in all possibilities. The gunas move as the wind moves in space. Practice is defined by the verse: evolution and involution. After balancing the body and breath we turn our focus inward. The gaze of the eyes in a hatha practice is captured by the word drishti—focused gaze. The one who sees is our real self. In hatha practice, our eyes are open but not playing among the senses. The gaze of eye provides a point of stillness, a developing point of reference, freed from the craving of the senses and mind.

Bless the eyes
For they are the gifts of angels,
For they tell the truth.
Mary Oliver

TECHNIQUE

Asanas and Their Benefits: Annamayakosha

Standing Poses - Annamayakosha

→ Strengthen body as you work against gravity.
→ Activate quadriceps, the largest muscle in the body, and hamstrings, the tightest group.
→ Create space for sciatic nerve, reducing threat of sciatica.
→ Lengthen and align spine to prepare for meditation.
→ Provide a sense of ground through legs, hips, and spine.
→ Develop postural alignment.
→ Teach full body awareness via neuro-anatomy of proprioception, and integration with visual, vestibular, and cerebellar functions.

Brahmana emphasized.

Standing Balance Poses - Annamayakosha

→ Help feet, ankles, and knees develop even strength, eliminating old habits of tension that prevent ease in standing and grounding.
→ Stretch and lubricate joints, tendons, and ligaments.
→ Open psoas and quadriceps musculature, bringing awareness to connection between torso and legs.
→ Teach awareness of lines of energy through body supported by correct alignment and stabilization of hips.
→ Alleviate knee pain.
→ Improve digestion and elimination by amplifying heat in the body.
→ Activate musculature that assists return of venal blood and lymph flow.
→ Teach full body awareness via neuro-anatomy of proprioception, and integration with feedback loops within visual, vestibular, and cerebellar functions.

Balance of brahmana and langhana.

Counterpose

The Sanskrit term *pratikriasana* means: against the action of the pose. A counterpose is an action that releases any possible strain of the previous poses. This is best understood by example. After a series of standing poses, the toxins stored in the muscle tissue as by-products of metabolism, such as lactic acid, are released into the intercellular fluids. Toxins need to move through the lymph system back to the heart to be purified out of the blood stream by the liver. Counterposes to a standing series are child's pose or hero, which squeeze and soften the muscle tissues of the legs, and inversions that help to drain the fluid in the legs. Simple *viparita karani,* with hips on a block and legs straight up, helps to drain fluid.

Preparation for Standing Poses: Hip ROM

We use the term Hip Range of Motion instead of Hip Openers. The movement of the hips is supported by the action of the thighs, core and back. We are looking for healthy movement. Actively stretching these muscles is more helpful for our hips than passively stretching them. A passive stretch may lengthen the ligaments of the pelvis. We want to protect the ligaments of the pelvis by not overstretching them.

sacrum

Movements of the Bones

The movements of the sacrum, the series of fused vertebrae between the hips at the base of the spine, are called nutation and counter-nutation. Nutation means that the sacrum "nods" forward. Counter-nutation is the opposite. Both these actions are guided by the muscle group called the ilio-psoas, a combination of the iliacus that connects the inner hip to the inner thigh and the psoas that connects the lumbar spine to the inner thigh. The combined contraction is nutation. The combined extension is counter-nutation ("a"). But they also function separately. The iliacus can be in nutation and the psoas in counter-nutation ("b"). This requires the strong paired action of the transversus abdominis at the lower core and the gluteus medius on the outer hip.

Nutation		Counter-nutation "a" and "b"	
Cow *iliacus and psoas contract*		**Cat ("a")** *iliacus and psoas lengthen*	
Down dog *First teach sacrum nods*		**Down dog ("b")** *aligned iliacus contracts psoas extends*	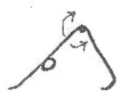

Chair pose teaches this action of the transversus abdominis and the gluteus medius and the simultaneous activation of *mula bandha*.

Mula bandha is separate from aswini mudra, activated by the muscles of the sphincter. To understand nutation and counter-nutation further, here is the pelvic floor. On the pelvic floor there are two triangles that tip away from the base of the ischial tuberosities.

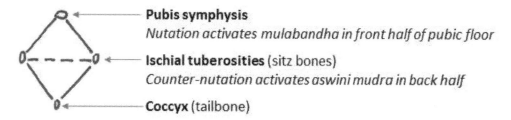

Pubis symphysis
Nutation activates mulabandha in front half of pubic floor

Ischial tuberosities (sitz bones)
Counter-nutation activates aswini mudra in back half

Coccyx (tailbone)

Additionally, during nutation, the ischial tuberosities (sitz bones) move farther apart. When the sacrum counternutates, the sitz bones draw closer together. Simultaneously, the iliac crests move in reverse, closer when the base widens and apart when the base narrows.

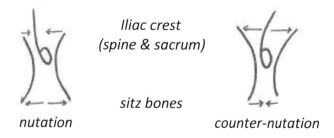

*Iliac crest
(spine & sacrum)*

sitz bones

nutation   *counter-nutation*

In chair pose and in many standing poses, we activate the counternutation "b." In this case, the sitz bones are more neutral. The neutral position of the sitz bones results from the strenuous activation of the lower core against the sturdy support of the back muscles.

The hips tilt forward and back together and separately, by virtue of the sacro-illiac joints (S-I). The S-I- joints, where the hips attach to the sacrum, are shaped like ears, and are not much different in size. If you have seen a dog perk up his ears and move them separately to locate sound, you can imagine how the hips move separately to support the extension and flexion of the thighs as we walk. In the standing warrior poses, the S-I joints are used in opposition, giving them full range of motion and thereby keeping them mobile.

In Warrior II the action of the bandhas assists counter-nutation. Our natural tendency is to nutate in this pose because of the bend in the front leg and because of the pull of the femur to the rear of the mat in the back leg.

This diagram is a review of the natural curves of the spine and the effect of the bandhas to support the spine. Notice that all bandhas lift the spine from the front. The back muscles meet that lift by engaging to hold steady.

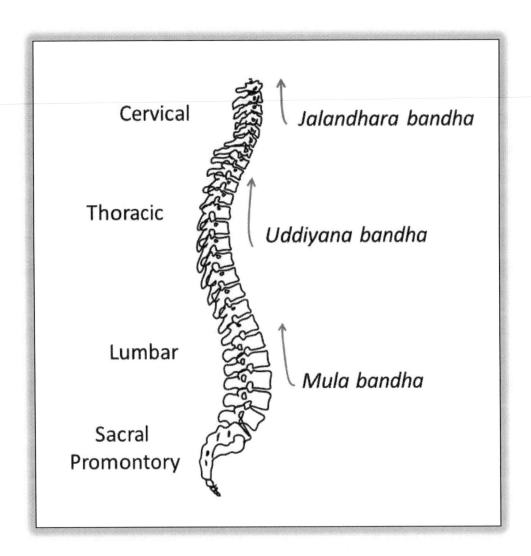

Hip ROM Series on the Back

1 - Knees to chest: alternately   *together*

2 - Strengthen with resistance:
  extending arms inside the legs   *and outside*

This action presses the sacrum down and activates a healthy neutral spine.

3 - Knees circles   *hold ankles with knees apart*   *supine pose*

4 - Legs lifts

5 - One leg abduction and adduction with   *6 - Full circumduction*
   other leg bent to the side:
   hips level   *hips stacked*
                                   engage core
                                   into upper hip

Standing Poses and Deep Relaxation

Foot position
- Outer edges of feet aligned
- In wide stance forward fold, toes angle in to help adductors lengthen, and to assist nutation of the sacrum.
- In warrior poses the heels are aligned, or in a modified stance separate the heels to the sides of the mat.
- In warrior I, the back foot aims to the front corner of the mat to assist the alignment of the hips to the front of the mat.
- In warrior II, the back foot is more parallel to the back edge of the mat and the stance can be wider.

Feet, legs & hips support spine and breath
The action of the feet and legs supports the lower spine. This frees the upper spine to move with an open diaphragmatic breath.

Shoulders & arms support breath and spine
The action of the arms supports an open chest and an aligned spine, helping the breath stay steady and full. The scapulae anchor behind the ribs via the combined action of the lower trapezius, the serratus anterior and rhomboids.

Deep relaxation
The energy generated by the standing poses, enhanced by full breaths and directed to all parts of the body, leads to a vibrant deep relaxation. The rajoguni nature of a standing practice lifts us far from the pull of tamoguna and allows us to float in a sattvic state of relaxation. Our responsibility as teachers is to guide our students into a calm focused mental state, gradually centering them on the sensations of breathing as the physical body settles. The centering effect will take students inward toward their I-am, their simple existence freed from the boundaries of identification.

Simple verbal cues:

- → Let the body be heavy. Follow the exhaling phase of breath.
- → Now while inhaling, notice the buoyancy that comes with breathing.
- → Trace the movement and sensations of breathing in through the nostrils and back out.
- → Feel the rising and falling of the abdomen.
- → Listen to the quiet sound breathing, the sound of a distant surf.

And give them time in silence.

Sequencing: How Standing Poses Teach One Another

Gateway poses
These four poses stabilize or release the action of the standing poses

Mountain	*Wide stance Forward Fold*	*Chair*	*Downward Facing Dog*

Integrates	Releases hamstrings, adductors, core, back	Strengthens hamstrings, adductors, core, back	Stabilizes shoulders, and hips

The muscle action of a standing pose becomes the basis for the next pose.

Warrior I

Teaches internal rotation of back thigh, front knee alignment

Warrior II

Deepens with internal rotation of back thigh; maintain knee alignment

Upward Warrior

Open front lateral Spine

Front leg stretch

Extend hamstrings of front leg

Triangle

Keep lateral spine open and extended front leg

Preparation for Rotated Triangle: 5 poses

Standing Crescent   *Cross prayer*   *Extended arms*

      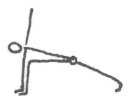

Extend leg and   maintain anchor   Align shoulders
anchor back foot   rotate and lengthen spine

Front leg stretch   *Rotated Triangle*

Lengthen hamstrings   anchor back leg heel
                           lengthen spine and align shoulders

Preparation for Rotated Standing Big Toe balance: 9 poses

On back, practice lengthening the ilio-tibial band attachments. As the I-T band lengthens the quadratus lumborum and the gluteus medius can release so the hip will move, and the spine can align. It will be helpful to isolate the gluteus medius from the gluteus maximus. An active gluteus maximus will prevent the hips from leveling when the leg is extended back.

Leg crossed   *Rotated belly*

   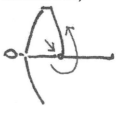

Drop hip of crossed leg   Cross leg to the opposite side,
                                 keep hip pulling away from shoulders
                                 via pectineus (short adductor)

Then standing:

Standing Tree

Femur externally rotates
via sartorius

Intense Big Toe stretch

Draw hip down via pectineus
while lifting leg

Dancer

Lengthen quad and
engage back
with core support

Half Moon

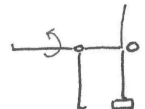

Femur externally rotates

Rotated half moon

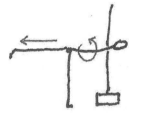

Hip drops, femur
internally rotates,
hamstrings engage

Warrior III

Level the hips,
activate hamstrings
and gluteus medius

Rotated Big Toe Balance

Hip of lifted leg pulls to floor
hamstrings of lower leg engage
with active core support

Each posture awakens a unique facet of the journey of self-discovery.
Le Page

PRACTICUM

Keep it Simple: Teaching Postures 101

Say the Pose	Say the Breath	Give 3 Cues

1. Observe the whole group and notice general patterns

2. Say the pose clearly: "Warrior 1"

3. Say the breath clearly: "Inhale"

4. Give 3 simple cues to set up the pose.

   1 - Ground your back heel
   2 - Rise up with your core
   3 - Lift arms overhead

5. While holding a pose, refine. You can teach to one or all layers of experience (koshas).
   a. Annamaya kosha (Gross: Physical body, senses)
      i. Establishing security
      ii. Alignment - start at the root/base and work your way up
      iii. Set up the pose
      iv. What is one cue for annamayakosha in Warrior 1?

   b. Pranamaya kosha (Gross: Breath, chakras)
      i. Start to shift awareness from the external experience to the inner body
      ii. Breath to tame the senses and "activate the value of the pose"
      iii. What is one cue for pranamayakosha in Warrior 1?

   c. Manomaya kosha (Subtle: mind, thought, emotion)
      i. Collecting info
      ii. Noticing habitual thought patterns and emotions
      iii. What is one cue for manomayakosha in Warrior 1?

    d. Vijnyanamaya kosha (Causal: witness, insight)
        i. Independent and unaffected by sensation and thought
        ii. Observing witness
        iii. What is learned by observing the outer three koshas?
            1. It is important to leave time/space for students to observe their experience
                a. Ex: Lie on back for a minute or two after Legs up the Wall
                b. Ex: Stand and feel L/R sides after balancing
        iv. What is one cue for vijnyanamayakosha in Warrior 1?

    e. Anandamaya kosha (Causal: True Self, Bliss)
        i. Cannot be taught, only experienced
        ii. Glimpses of this layer are most commonly experienced in savasana
        iii. What is one cue for anandamaya kosha in Warrior 1? Is there a cue for this layer?

FINAL THOUGHTS:
    → Hold the pose for an equal amount of time on each side.
    → Be unobtrusive.
       – Let the students experience themselves, not you
    → Breathe with the group.
    → Teach only what you yourself have experienced and know.

ANATOMY

Respiratory System

Breathing is central to life and to our well-being. The health of the body and the mind is supported by complete breath. Quite naturally, hatha yoga practice cultivates healthy breathing patterns by developing the primary and accessory muscles of breathing and by releasing tension associated with inhibition of breathing.

Respiration has two levels: the lungs and the pulmonary system. The lungs draw in air and expel it from the body. The heart and pulmonary system circulate oxygen, the return of carbon dioxide, and move other molecules of nutrition for metabolism.

Respiration is intimately linked with health. Respiration is one system that assists homeostasis. Homeostasis is the internal regulation of body functions including heart function, brain function, metabolism, endocrine balance, muscle and vascular health, and lymphatic drainage.

Shallow breathing is detrimental to health, and reduced movement in the lungs can create areas of stagnation that challenge the health of the body's tissues. Deep diaphragmatic breathing can increase the volume of air intake by 600%.

The main muscle of breathing is the diaphragm. The diaphragm has a hooded shape and is attached to the lumbar spine and the lower ribs. The central tendon of the diaphragm is not attached to any bone. It pulls on the pleura, the lining of the diaphragm, and creates a vacuum in the lungs that draws in the air. Other muscles stabilize posture so that the diaphragm has leverage. Accessory muscles on the dorsal side  include the latissimus dorsi and quadratus lumborum. On the ventral side, the upper ribs are stabilized by the pectoralis minor, and the abdomen supports a thoraco-diaphragmatic breath.

Movement of the entire abdominal cavity is included in breathing. Without that movement, the lungs could not open. The diaphragm is so neatly tucked into the body between the lungs and the abdominal cavity that it takes on the shape of contiguous organs. The support of the abdominal organs for the spine and the breath is a hydraulic action. The inner organs surrounded by the encasing of the peritoneum act as a water-balloon that changes shape as we move and breathe. The movement of this cavity is as essential to breathing as the opening of the lungs.

Opening the lower abdomen to create a relaxed breath is only the beginning of a complete breath. Then the lower ribs must open wide to enhance the function of the capillary-rich lower lobes of the lungs, and the upper chest must expand to fill the upper lobes. The two latter actions require the support of the abdominal sheath and the upper pectoralis muscles.

Opening up the breathing apparatus and finding appropriate support for deeper breathing during the day is a long-term goal of yoga. Other important focal points of breathing are the intercostal muscles and the scapulae. The intercostal muscles lie between the ribs. They are responsible for enhancing the capacity of breath and assisting with the movement of lymph, part of the immune system. Lateral bends help to open the ribs. Adhesions of the scapulae to the dorsal rib area can inhibit breathing. Working the range of motion through the arms assists with the full range of motion of the scapulae.

Accessory muscles of breathing
Assist the action of the diaphragm and the intercostals

- To stabilize the lower back: quadratus lumborum
- To stabilize the midback: latissimus dorsi, erector spinae
- To lower the scapulae: lower trapezius
- To stabilize the upper back: the rhomboids, serratus anterior
- To lift the chest: pectoralis minor, sternocleidomastoid, scalenes

Parts of the Respiratory System

- Nasal Cavities: Mucous membranes inside the nose warm the air.
- Cilia: Hair-like structures within the nasal cavities that filter incoming air.
- Mucus: A viscous fluid that facilitates the elimination of particulate matter trapped by the cilia.
- Trachea: A passage from the throat to the bronchial tubes in the lungs.
- Lungs: Here the bronchial tubes branch like a tree through diminishing sizes into tiny sacs called alveoli, where gaseous exchange occurs. Due to gravity, the lower lobes of each lung have a greater more capillary exchange than do the upper lobes.
- Diaphragm, ribs, and intercostal muscles: Work as a pump for the intake of oxygen and discharge of carbon dioxide. The heart and lungs are well protected within the thoracic cavity created by the ribs.

Breathing and the Nervous System
The tradition of hatha yoga has long known the effect of breathing on the nervous system and practiced methods to balance the autonomic nervous system by means of carefully extending the length of breath. The yogic teaching emphasizes a rest/action cycle associated with the rest action pulses of the heart and the shifting dominance of one nasal turbinate over the other. The nasal turbinate is a small scroll-like bone that

extends horizontally along the lateral wall of the nasal passage. One nostril has a greater air capacity over the other at any given time due to a shift in the position of these bones. Nostril dominance shifts from side to side every two hours. This subtle teaching of yoga is valued in Chinese medicine. Modern Science does not concur with the relation of nostril dominance to the circulation of energy and subsequent health of the body.

Benefits of *Pranayama* Practice[1]

- Increased blood flow in the capillaries (due to the size of the CO_2 molecule), and oxygenation of the blood with an even blood flow to the brain.
- Sympathetic and parasympathetic balance in the autonomic nervous system
- Deep abdominal breathing acts as a pump for the circulation of fluids to the organs of digestion, massaging the kidneys and facilitating peristalsis in the intestines.
- Within the immune system, the spleen, rich in lymphatic tissue and white blood cells, is massaged, assisting in the removal of dead red blood cells.
- The closest the body has to a lymphatic pump is the movement of the intercostal muscles while breathing. Abdominal-diaphragmatic breathing promotes lymphatic circulation.
- The enhanced movement of breathing also promotes venous return to the heart, and improves the gaseous exchange within the lungs. Both assist the work of the heart, thereby slowing heart rate.

Research on Yoga and Breathing:[2]

Slow, rhythmic, abdominal-diaphragmatic breathing leads to an increase in CO2 (carbon dioxide) in the arteries, which, in turn, lowers blood pH. This lowered pH relaxes/dilates the blood vessels, which then increases blood flow and oxygenation to the brain and other regions of body. This increased circulation removes metabolites and increases the transfer of O2 into cellular tissues. Although it seems counterintuitive, it is this increase in CO2 that actually increases O2 availability in cells.

On the other hand, chest breathing (aka hyperventilation) leads to a lowering of CO2 levels in arteries, which signals the blood vessels to constrict, thereby lowering circulation. Chest breathing creates a reduction in availability of O2 in body's tissues, including the brain. (See diagram on the next page.)

---

[1] Within the manual, *pranayama* is discussed in the Philosophy section, Sāmkhya *sutra* 5, and in Technique, "Teaching *Pranayama*."
[2] *The Journal of the International Association of Yoga Therapists*, Vol 2, No. 1, 1991. "The Psychophysiology of Respiration," Richard Miller, Ph.d.

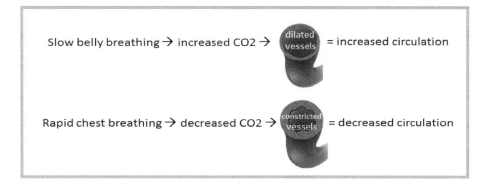

Slow belly breathing → increased CO2 → dilated vessels = increased circulation

Rapid chest breathing → decreased CO2 → constricted vessels = decreased circulation

Inhalation: The powerful Descending Movement of the Diaphragm

- O_2-rich air is pulled to the lower lobes of the lungs where greater O_2/CO_2 exchange is possible. The lower lobes of the lungs are richer in blood and capillaries.
- The downward movement stimulates peristalsis of the stomach and intestines, and massages the liver.
- The pericardium of the heart is attached to the diaphragm and is massaged during inhalation.

Exhalation: The Powerful Ascending Force of the Diaphragm

- The movement assists venous return and promotes lymphatic circulation.
- The movement is associated with the shift of the autonomic nervous system from sympathetic arousal to parasympathetic relaxation. This shift means the body is moving toward reduced heart rate, breath rate, and O_2 consumption. Reduced blood sugar levels and blood lactate, and reduced muscle tension occur with a reduction in sympathetic arousal.

Personality and Behavior Traits Correlated with Breathing Patterns

- Clinical symptoms of passive and dependent behaviors are correlated with thoracic breathing, rapid breath rate, and decreased CO_2. Respiration patterns return to normal as behaviors change.
- Hyperventilation syndrome is associated with acute anxiety attacks.
- Abdominal-diaphragmatic breath is associated with decreased fatigue, anxiety, depression and mood disturbances.
- Intellectual, emotional, and physical health are associated with large tidal volume and elevated CO_2.

Cardio-vascular System[3]

Circulation naturally increases as a result of stretching and squeezing the body during *hatha yoga* practice. The circulatory system carries oxygen from the lungs and nutrients from the stomach and small intestines throughout the body. Waste products of metabolism are delivered to the lungs, skin, and kidneys to be expelled outside the body. The circulatory system also serves as a pathway for the distribution of hormones and neuropeptides produced by the brain and other organs of the endocrine system. Circulation of blood assists the maintenance of body temperature.

Parts of the Circulatory System

- Heart: A fist-sized striated muscle inside the rib cage, tilted slightly left of center, which pumps blood to the whole body by virtue of pressure created by cardiac contraction. Smooth muscles in the arteries and assist the movement of blood volume. Deoxygenated blood comes to the right side of the heart, and goes back to the lungs. Oxygenated blood from the lungs goes to the left atrium and out the left ventricle under relatively high pressure. The left side is more muscular.

- Arteries: Muscular blood vessels that carry oxygenated blood. The aorta comes out of the left ventricle. When the main arteries of the heart that are clogged, by-pass surgery is indicated.

- Veins: Thin-walled vessels that return deoxygenated blood. Veins have valves that prevent back flow. Exercise assists venous return.

- Capillaries: Small, thin-walled vessels between arteries and veins where the exchange of nutrients, O_2 and waste products takes place between cells and circulatory system.

- Three main blood cells:
  - Red carries oxygen and other nutrients to body tissue.
  - White is involved with immune response and phagocytosis.
  - Platelets are responsible for clotting.

The Work of the Heart
Every minute, the blood supply makes a complete cycle through the heart.

The heart rests while on the job. The systolic (contraction) phase is half the length of the diastolic, which is the relaxation phase. The ratios developed in yogic breathing are based on the contraction and relaxation phases of the heart. A 1:2 ratio is commonly used.

The heart has an internal conduction system that is coordinated with autonomic control.

---

[3] Joseph Le Page developed his ideas around therapeutic yoga while helping heart patients in recovery.

During a stress response, elevated heart rate and increased blood pressure are key to survival. This results from activation of the sympathetic division of the autonomic nervous system.[4] When the body shifts back to rest, in that state the parasympathetic division predominates by way of the vagus nerve.[5] Its transmitter is acetylcholine (ACH), one that is quickly deactivated by reabsorption.

Yoga and Heart Disease

Inversions are contraindicated for heart disease. The pressure of the reverse in blood flow can elevate blood pressure. However, a gradual introduction of change, such as legs up the wall or on a chair can begin to reverse the condition. The carotid artery in the neck monitors blood flow to the brain. For a healthy circulatory system, the inversion is an ideal way to assist lowering blood pressure. When the carotid artery detects the increase in pressure, it signals the body to reduce the blood flow to the brain, thereby adjusting the overall blood pressure in the body toward reduction.

Gentle yoga and breathing exercises are valuable for all heart patients. The practice provides a ground for lifestyle change by encouraging a relationship with the environment that is not a response to threat.[6]

Breathing Exercises and the Heart
- *Nadhi Shodhana* balances the sympathetic and parasympathetic divisions of the autonomic nervous system.
- *Bastrika* energizes the heart.
- A longer exhale than inhale (2:1) lowers the heart rate and, subsequently, the breathing rate.

Conditions of the Circulatory System
- Hypertension: There is no well-defined organic cause in the majority of cases. An over-activation of sympathetic arousal is the main contributing factor. The blood pressure maintains a higher baseline functioning. Narrowing of arteries worsens the condition as in cholesterol blocking.

- Coronary Heart Disease: Lack of exercise, smoking, processed foods, and a high stress contribute to this condition. Atherosclerosis is plaque formation on the inside of the artery walls. Contributing factors include cholesterol. Buildup research is advancing, but contributing factors are not well understood. Cholesterol filled arteries block the free flow of blood so the heart has to work harder.

---

[4] See Physiology and Homeostasis.
[5] The vagus nerve is covered in more detail in Chapter 7.
[6] *The Program for Reversing Heart Disease*, by Dr. Dean Ornish, involves lifestyle changes toward a vegetarian diet and yoga.

- **Stroke**: A degenerative vascular disorder in which the vascular system to the brain is damaged. The brain is dead after 10-12 minutes of oxygen deprivation.

- **Varicose Veins**: Hereditary factors and/or a sedentary lifestyle disrupt the effect of the venous valves in the legs that are assisted by muscular contraction. Abdominal pressure through *uddiyana bandha* can assist venous return.

ASSIMILATION

Content

➢ Describe three key aspects of "elegant" sequencing and why they are important.

➢ What makes the heart and lungs companion systems?

➢ What do we know about breath rhythms and heart function?

➢ How does the practice of yoga take advantage of that fact to improve both systems?

➢ The diaphragm shares the attachment of its lower tendons on the site of the lumbar spine with what key muscle(s) of the lower abdomen that assist movement?

Contemplation

➢ How do you experience the gunas in the standing poses? Base, movement and learning?

➢ Which guna do you favor when you practice standing poses?

➢ Which guna might you favor as you teach standing poses?

Personal practice

➢ How does your personal practice feel as you add standing poses?

➢ Describe in terms of langhana and brahmana.

Poses

➢ Draw three sequences of standing poses.

➢ Add counterposes. What muscle action in the body needs to be neutralized?

Yoga becomes the destroyer of sorrows in one who is
temperate in food and recreation, balanced in actions,
and moderate in sleep and wakefulness.
Bhagavad Gita 6/17

Chapter Five – Suffering

SS 7 & 12 Suffering & the Five Knots of False knowledge
YS II/3 – 11 Klesas
Begin written assignment on the Klesas
Begin Poses papers
Choose a topic for the Value of Yoga paper

The story of the fifth chapter: the heart of self-care is managing our suffering. To help ourselves and our students, we seek self-knowledge, and self-attribution. Staying a victim will keep us in suffering. Finding freedom lies in mastering a self-discipline that enhances our strengths, minimizes our weaknesses and connects us to a deep source of seeing, knowing and wholeness. Within asana, we look carefully at back care and abdominal strengtheners, common areas of weakness that are effectively addressed with practice.

Contents

PHILOSOPHY

Sutra 7: Suffering Due to Self, Other Beings and the Divine World

The three kinds of suffering are graded into categories related with the *gunas*. The grossest level of the projection of energy is the primordial elements, the *bhutas*; any creature or individual has a form due to the elements. Gross forms cause us suffering, whether a tiny virus, a rabid animal, or a car accident.

The divine world refers to the most pure or *sattvic* projection of energy. In this tradition, earth, water, fire, air and space as they express as oceans, winds, floods, and fire can bring enormous devastation. Why these forces are divine is because their whole existence is for others. Fire, water and air sustain the life of all beings, and have no needs of their own.

Human life is the expression of *rajoguna*, and naturally this expression includes the three qualities from gross to subtle. We suffer due to ourselves in three ways: illness of the body, weakness of the mind, and impurity of the intellect. Yoga practice addresses these through *asana*, *pranayama*, and meditation. Suffering due to the imposition of other beings and the devastations of natural disasters cannot be avoided, but the effects are tempered by the inner strength of detachment.

What is subtler is more powerful. We can sustain injury to the body better than to our emotions. The most dangerous of all devastations is based in impurity of the human intellect. One charismatic politician, one religious leader, one dictator can propel large populations into suffering. The belief in accumulation, shared by many, is leading to large imbalances among people and in the environment. Our own impurity is called wrong knowledge and it keeps us in bondage.

In Samkhya sutra 12, wrong knowledge and suffering are further explained (also covered in chapter 10). Suffering is due to the identification of self with the fluctuations of energy, thereby creating bondage. Freedom comes with finding the self as seer and knower, unchanging and blissful.

Sutra 12: The Five Knots of False Knowledge

Darkness, infatuation, great infatuation, aversion, and blind aversion bind us to ignorance of the real self. Darkness of disconnection with the source covers the intellect. Then the ego becomes infatuated with itself, since it does not see its source in light and knowledge. Then attraction to outward objects and relationships take precedence over the real self. With attractions come aversion, and fear of loss, and finally the great fear of death.

The Five Knots of False Knowledge, also Patanjali's Klesas, the Miseries   (Y.S. II/3-11)

Avidya	Attaching the purity of seeing to the fluctuations of the seen, and believing that the seen is all that there is
Asmita	Asserting the ascendancy of the ego, the I-am, as the center of our being and believing that our intelligence is our own
Raga	Attractions
Dvesa	Repulsions
Abhinevesa	Desire for life, and fear of loss of control and death

---

According to Sāmkhya and Yoga, what makes the path integrative is finding the seer, and separating out the seer from the seen. When we identify ourselves with the seen (sanyoga) we feel a sense of separation from self, and we gather all the attendant feelings of being disconnected, dismembered, diseased, and distracted. When we come closer to the seer (yoga) we feel integrated. The separation of seer and seen (viyoga) is needed. The self we seek is consciousness itself.

TECHNIQUE

Asanas and Their Benefits: Annamayakosha & Backbends

Backbends - Annamayakosha

→ Massage back muscles and invigorate digestive organs.
→ Remove stiffness from cervical, thoracic and lumbar regions.
→ Energize pituitary, parathyroid, thyroid, and adrenal glands.
→ Squeeze kidneys and adrenals.
→ Increase energy from hormone balance and stimulate nervous system.
→ Increase lung capacity.
→ Relieve asthma and respiratory problems.

Brahmana emphasized.

Sequence for Back Care & Abdominal Strengtheners

A healthy back relies on a healthy core; thus for back care we need core strengtheners. Also, we need a general understanding of our back: isolate areas of trouble and learn how to address them. Regular back care increases the articulation of the back muscles individually, and helps us feel how they work together in mutual support.

Know your back:

Areas of chronic tension   Patterns of movement

Lordosis   Kyphosis   Scoliosis

Spine functions   Nervous system   Weight bearing

Front – autonomic activity… excitation & relaxation
Back – muscular movement… volition… patterns of movement / mind

Remedy: length + strength = flexible strength

Movement with breath: Vinyasa

Breath increases O2.
Increased blood flow reduces contraction and interrupts "pain-contraction-pain" cycle.

Patterns in the body have a mental correlate related with breath.
Increasing breathing reduces effect of conditioning.

Poses:

Roll spine front to back
Thumb breathing

side to side
standing
half moon

exhale   *inhale*

Seated

half moon

exhale   *inhale*

Cat / Cow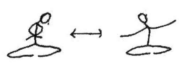

C-curve
(from table)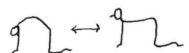

Low back lengthening

Table   Extended child's

inhale   *exhale*

Wood chopper

inhale   *exhale*

with shoulders

Wall hang

Breath of joy

exhale   *inhale...   more...   more*

Abdominal Strengthening

Pelvic rock   and lifts   with arms

inhale   *exhale*   *exhale*   *inhale*   *exhale*

Knee to chest   Breathing egg

exhale   *inhale*

For the Back on the Belly... keep belly traveling toward the spine

Cobra   Boat   Sphinx   with bent legs

Leg lifts   close   and   wide

Release in extended child's pose as you go...

Standing Lunges
Moderate lunge stance
one leg forward
same side arm behind back

129

with opposite arm raised – shoulders low

inhale   *exhale*   *inhale*   *exhale*

SPECIAL NEEDS:

Scoliosis – unilateral poses

Tiger stretch   Sunbird

exhale   *inhale*   *exhale*   *inhale*

Lengthen sides   seated   standing

Seated Twists   bow to easy side   twist

Sciatica – modifications

Forward fold to a right angle only   or with bent knees
Strength on belly (see above poses)...   release back

Sacroiliac Joint

Supine bound angle pose   raising legs slowly

Standing modification for all back conditions

shorter stance   back foot out to side

During any and all sessions..
take time to counterpose

Restorative: legs up wall

Abdominal Strengtheners

1. Breathing with leg (5x)

inhale *exhale*

2. Knee to chest pose

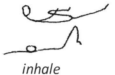

3. Crunches (6x)

inhale *exhale*

4. Crossing median... hold (2x)

5. Rapid knee to chest (20x)

exhale *inhale switch*

6. Legs away – legs over with crossed ankles (5x)

7. Obliques – legs and arms up
   hold head up and arms to one side (7x)

8. "Clock" spinal twist

9. Lumbar twist

inhale *exhale*

10. Knee to chest release... rock spine up

11. Reverse table... tuck tailbone

12. Hips to heels and slow roll down...
    swipe hands on legs

13. Deep relaxation

Elements of a Backbend: Quadriceps, Shoulders and a Long Core

Two-legged table

lengthen quads in eccentric contraction
internal rotation of thighs
draw kneecaps toward feet
engage core toward head

Draw one arm back

inhale open   *exhale down*
open pecs in upper chest

Bridge

open pecs further by engaging arms into ground
adding use of rhomboids, erector spinae
and lower trapezius

Lying bound angle pose

with deep breathing,
lengthen core

Supported bridge

additional lengthening of core

Twist

counterpose

Deep relaxation

drop thighs and shoulders
observe undulation of spine with breathing

Yoga practice is like taming a lion. A lion cannot be tamed in one day;
but slowly, gently and lovingly, it can be tamed.
If any harsh tactics are used, it will be furious
and will attack in an attempt to protect itself.
Swami Bawra

METHOD

Working with the Edges[1]

Why is it important to work with edges?

Yoga therapy means that we are helping students get the most out of their yoga practice. Giving them information on the benefits of poses and providing hand-outs is useful but we risk putting ourselves as teachers into the role of fixers. How can we empower students to help themselves? One of the most effective ways is to teach them to notice, think about, and work with their own edges. This is an internal focus that is sometimes compromised by large classes and instructors who roam the room adjusting poses. Students need a way to be their own instructors. Our job is to teach them to turn their focus and observation inward and explore the knowledge that can be gained there.

Tarcher Putnam writes in *Living Yoga*, "If I never explore my limits, my body-mind will gradually tighten and become unconscious. If I regularly explore my limits in a caring and adventuresome fashion, I will expand and grow in a vital fashion. But if I try to push myself past where I am honestly able to go, I will probably be met by pain and disease."

Why is it difficult for students?

Some new yoga students do not rush deeply into postures. But because of our cultural conditioning, many are overly ambitious. It is a shock for them to learn how different yoga is. We do not work with the "no pain no gain" adage. In traditional fitness activities, the goal is to exhaust the body – working the body/muscles until you feel you cannot lift one more weight or do one more jumping jack. Following an exhausting workout, the muscles need rest and recuperation to regenerate muscle fibers, only to begin the process again a day or two later.

One fitness article I read noted the distinction between one's "mental edge" and "physical edge," pointing out that "your mental edge is the preconceived notion of what your body is capable of doing, while your physical edge is what your body can actually do." With *hatha* practice, we work to eliminate this distinction. We bring the mental and physical edges together so they work in unison.

---

[1] Original paper written by Lisa Thiel, BYT 500, E-RYT 500

It is difficult to overcome our culture's competitive conditioning. It takes a lot of courage for students, who are so used to judging and pushing themselves and comparing to others, to begin tuning out the external and turning, instead, inwards. Observation of limitations without self-judgment is not easy. And comparison of oneself with others is not easy to avoid when observing someone else's prefect handstand. Teachers themselves often demonstrate their abilities. For a useful self-awareness to develop, we need to encourage a healthy witness consciousness.

Newer yoga students, for their own various reasons or fears, minimize emotions that they might feel. As such, they might be afraid to get to know themselves through their yoga practice. They might be afraid to experience emotions and uncover the traces of previous experiences hidden deep within. Even teachers avoid their emotions, instead deflecting back to their interest in the physicality of the poses.

Techniques for use in class
Here is a list of ways to help students find and work with their edges so that practice can become therapeutic:

→ *Breath...* Repeatedly remind students of their breath; synchronize breath with movement, and movement with breath. This practice assists turning inward and minimizes looking around and "competing" for the best pose. Breathing helps instruct the poses by creating varying sensations in both the inhaling and exhaling phases. Breathing gives a focal point to initiate the process of listening to oneself and learning from oneself. Exhaling deeply helps the body to soften into the stretch, assisting the ability to find the healthy edges of the postures.

→ *Talk of the stretch reflex...* The stretch reflex is the contraction initiated in the muscle belly in response to stretching. It is a valuable protective mechanism. Teaching students about the stretch reflex helps to adjust their mindset regarding the need to push to achieve fitness goals. We are not simple avoiding discomfort. We are looking for the edges that are signaled by this stretch reflex. There are actual signposts to heed. Erich Schiffmann in his book, *Moving into Stillness*, suggests that people too often neglect these signs and therefore act as though "one foot is on the accelerator and one is on the brake." Progress is made when we understand when to deepen and when to stay as we are and simply breathe.

→ *Closing the eyes...* I frequently suggest that my students close their eyes. Some newer students find this very difficult at first, and can find only brief moments of closing the eyes more beneficial until they feel more comfortable. This helps to avoid comparison and encourages inwardness, listening.

→ **Yield...** Donna Farhi has offered seven moving principles (as presented in Chapter 1). Her second principle, "yielding," helps students to orient to their bodies, to their own weight and to the space around them.

→ **Notice the effects...** It is useful to offer the pause, the opportunity for students to do a body scan after completing the first side of a posture, and to compare their sensations with the other side. This helps them discern the benefits of the poses for themselves.

→ **Intentions...** In a quiet moment at the beginning of class, have students explore their reasons for coming and then set a simple intention for that day. This helps to orient to the personal value of their practice.

→ **Apply 10% effort...** A fellow teacher, Michael Curtis has suggested the practice of starting off with 10% effort. The remaining 90% is breathing and awareness. We can incrementally add movement. This instruction helps the "expert" refrain from jumping ahead and the "china doll" feel less fear regarding the poses.

→ **Clear talk about edges...** Remind your students of how personal their own edges are. Language such as, "only you can know" where and when to move more deeply. Using words and phrases such as, "snuggle up to," "explore," "meet," and "get to know your edges" helps. Continually establish a healthy balance between pushing to fitness limits and being overly gentle and cautious. It is the students' "job" to find their own therapeutic edge within the work.

→ **Edges as a bubble...** Imagine being inside of a bubble and very gently working on expansion by pressing slightly, seeing what happens, and then testing the edge some more. Breathing well creates subtle movement.

→ **Sthira sukha...** the heart of asana practice. "Stable and easy" is a phrase that suits the exploration of each pose. Using this phrase as a guide, we can explore where a pose is strained or uncomfortable and bring more ease without losing dynamic stability.

→ While taming a lion, we cannot be overly cautious and gentle, nor can we be too forceful. We have to strike a firm balance: observe our limits, stay there, and then forge ahead when the body is ready to yield.

Assisting with Touch

Touch is integral to our body's self-awareness. Ways of "touching" that we have in the musculo-skeletal system are receptors embedded in the muscles and tendons, and receptors for proprioception in the joints (spatial orientation). They are part of our somato-sensory system. That is, information comes from our soma (body) to the brain and is received on the same part of the cortex as information from the skin regarding pain, temperature, light and deep touch. Skin, muscle-tendon sense, and proprioception comprise body awareness.

During a yoga session, when we touch a student with our hands, we are adding to their already enlivened system of feeling that is going on in the body. They are in a state of heightened touch experience before you add your hand. Consider this before you add the information that comes from your hand. Touch is part of learning effective movement, and a little touch goes a long way.

We do not often contemplate the power of touch. Without deep touch and pain receptors, we would crash around in our environment at great risk to our health and well-being. There are individuals who lack pain reception and, as children, they frequently break bones. Deep touch/pain receptors send their neuronal impulses to the brain with more synapses than light touch. Because of the survival need for immediate responses to pain, the possibility for other connections is wired into the nervous system. Light touch is different. There are fewer synaptic connections, which make the information travel more quickly to the brain. Think of the difference between playing a violin and touching a hot stove.

Assisting with touch:
  ➢ *Where is the action in the pose?*
  ➢ *Where is the action missing?*
  ➢ *Where is the student's experience unconscious?*

These are guiding questions for assisting. How can you stimulate an inner dialogue with your touch, rather than imposing the "correct" posture?

Let your intention be very clear in your mind. Without that clear intention, there is no purpose in touching. Your visualization should be distinct, but be careful that your touch has no intention of correcting your students with the "shoulds." Those are for you to carry. You should be careful. Assisting with touch comes second to verbal instruction and is used where verbal instruction and appropriate sequencing fall short. Challenge yourself to find the verbal instruction and the sequencing that will give them an "aha" experience that is theirs and not yours.

Why? Most people have a history with touch, and you do not know into what you are reaching: injuries, abuse, lack of enough touch. Your touch may be healing, but let the experience be about their need and not yours. Less is more in a situation where intimacy is heightened.

Effective verbal instruction empowers the students to find their way.

PRACTICUM

Keep it Simple: Tips for Touch

- Take a moment before teaching to set your intention to serve.

- Approach all adjustments with a clear intention, compassion, awareness and deep respect. Adjust with 100% attention EVERY TIME.

- Ask permission of the whole group before class, or individually and softly to that person.

- Touch like a wave: move in slow, be firm, and release slowly

- Be firm. Soft touch can be misleading or confusing

- Remember, assisting is enhancement not a correction of their experience, unless they are unsafe.

- If giving an assist to one side, try to return to assist the other side.

- Watch the student's face for discomfort, and keep an eye out for other non-verbal cues as well, such as crossing arms over the chest in a protective manner. Learn to sense when touch is probably not welcomed.

- Keep in mind that, often, students returning to or just beginning yoga after a serious illness or injury prefer not to be touched.

- Remember that assists are individually tailored for each student. Practice feeling for surrender. Practice feeling for resistance.

- Watch your thinking and your own insecurities—these are translated into touch.

- Physical areas to avoid: Belly, upper inner thighs, armpits or anywhere close to the breast in women.

ASSIMILATION

Content

➢ Is backbend a useful term?

➢ What three areas of our muscular-skeletal system have to extend open and strengthen to make backbending a useful practice for the spine?

➢ Learn and list the abdominal muscles and their primary action(s).

Contemplation

➢ Why is self-care and safe backbending included with the Samkhya Sutra that introduces the nature of suffering?

➢ What is the difference between suffering and pain?

➢ Consider a good assist that you have received in a class. What made it work?

Personal Practice

➢ Develop a backbending practice by attending to the three areas of the body that need to open and strengthen.

➢ Does personal practice help to alleviate any areas of your suffering?

Poses

➢ Draw a sequence that prepares your body for backbending.

➢ Draw arrows of movement where you go in and out of one pose or between two poses.

➢ Draw the action of breathing (when to inhale or exhale) and use of core.

➢ Draw some abdominal strengthening movements.

➢   Sketch the shapes of the spine below: What poses address each?

Lordosis:
*exaggerated
lumbar curve*

Kyphosis:
*exaggerated
thoracic curve*

Scoliosis:
*lateral bend
in spine*

One should raise the self by his own mind and not allow the self to sink;
for the mind alone is the friend of the self
and the mind alone is the foe of the self.
Bhagavad Gita 6/5

Chapter Six – Practice

SS 8 – 9 The Five Sources of Knowledge and the Five Causes of Action
YS I/1-16 The Five Modes of chitta, Practice with detachment
Written assignment due on the Klesas
Begin research on the Nervous System, the Brain, Yoga and Meditation
Continue Poses papers: Adding to Annamayakosha.
Plan your internship setting and time.

The story of the seventh chapter: We actively train our nervous system to sustain wholeness. The knowledge and experience of healthy choices can lead to further actions based on knowledge. In asana, we move to inversions, which enhance the health of the joints and sustain a vibrant physiology.

Contents

PHILOSOPHY

Samkhya Sutra 8: The Five Sources of Knowledge

There are five sources of knowledge, the five *buddhis*: the intellect, ego, mind, the five cognitive senses, and the five active senses. The word for intellect is also *buddhi*. According to Sāmkhya and Yoga, all instruments of nature are for learning and emancipation rather than enjoyment. *Bhoga* means enjoyment through experience. Yoga means liberation through experience. Ultimately, liberation comes with purity of the intellect, which guides our practice with discernment and reflects the pure light of consciousness. Instruments that have been developed through the evolutionary process of nature can now be refined through our yoga practice.

The five cognitive senses are hearing, touch, sight, taste, and smell, related with the elements of space, air, fire, water, and earth, respectively.[1] The organs of action are also correlated with the five elements. Our tongue and mouth create sound and speech. Our hands participate with touch and the element of air. Our legs move us forward when our eyes are focused with the help of light. Our generative organs are stimulated through the tongue and function through a watery medium. Smell and the earth element are connected with elimination.

All parts of our personalities are present on the yoga mat during practice. Some are contained like elimination and generation. That containment is part of practice. Practice includes all sources of knowledge; the placement of our feet and the gaze of the eyes are present along with a focused mind, a vital heart, and a discerning intellect. The goal is the refinement of all instruments of gaining knowledge, and by implication, we are turning them into instruments for gaining knowledge rather than keeping them as a means to fulfill desires. The resulting relaxation of craving moves us toward healthy detachment. The relief from the clamoring needs of the possessive mind and the move to observe and learn from experience deepens during relaxation and helps us surrender into a more authentic and real sense of self.

---

[1] *Kapil's Samkhya Patanjali's Yoga, sutras* 2 & 3.

Eightfold Nature	Sixteen Modifications		
Prakriti			
Intellect (buddhi/chitta)			
Ego		Mind	
Sound	Space/Ether	Ears	Mouth/Tongue
Touch	Air	Skin/Proprioception[2]	Hands
Sight	Fire	Eyes	Legs
Taste	Water	Tongue	Generative & Eliminative Organs
Smell	Earth	Nose	
Tanmatras	*Bhutas* 5 Primordial Elements	*Indriyas* 5 Cognitive Senses	*Indriyas* 5 Active Senses

Samkhya indicates a hierarchy within the five sources of knowledge—all sources are not created equal. The *buddhi* or *chitta* is the place from where the others sprout, the place where our learning is maintained, and the ultimate place of freedom.

---

[2] Proprioceptors are sensory receptors in muscles, tendons, and joints that respond to movement and assist spatial orientation. (More detail presented later in this chapter in the Anatomy section.)

Samkhya Sutra 9: The Five Causes of Action

These five are states of the intellect: evidence, fallacy, fancy, sleep and memory. We act based on the content of our *buddhi*, our intellect. Evidence is often called right knowledge; it is accurate perception and comprehension. Fallacy is a wrong perception; it is imagination or speculation. Sleep is a dull state of the intellect, and memory is a trace of previous experience that determines our action. Mostly we live in ignorance of truth and we are prompted by fallacy and fancy. Truth means we understand the real nature of the self as consciousness, not energy.

The instruments of gaining knowledge are activated by the twins of thought and breath. Five different states of our intellect shape our reality and therefore cause our action, and each state of the intellect is supported by breath or energy as the means to pursue the desired path of action.

Patanjali's Five Modes of Chitta, and Practice with Detachment

Patanjali also emphasizes these five states of the intellect and calls them the five *chitta-vrittis*. *Chitta-vrittis* are fluctuations or differing modes of the *chitta,* the place of intelligence. Patanjali presents them in his first chapter, just prior to the first method of practice with detachment.

Readiness

Atha samadhi-padah

I. Now, cognitive-absorption chapter.

> This first chapter is on the deep state of absorption called *samadhi.* The highest teaching comes first.

Atha yoganushaasanam

I/1 Now, yoga instruction.

> "Now" indicates the readiness of the teacher and the student.

Definition of Yoga

Yogas chitta-vritti-nirodhah

I/2 Yoga is *chitta-vritti* stillness.

> This well-known verse contains the essence of yoga practice. *Chitta-vritti* is commonly translated as mind, or thought-waves. *Vritti* means fluctuation, but *chitta* is the unique term that has no corresponding meaning in English. It is causal energy that lies in a specific place in the body that has the ability to capture and transmit the values of consciousness. The *chitta* modifies into the conscious intellect, ego, and mind.

Seer and seen

Tada drastuh svarupe 'vasthaanam

I/3 Then, of the seer, in one's own nature there is abidance.

> Once the fluctuations of *chitta* are stilled, consciousness is experienced as the self with its qualities of existence, knowledge, and infinity or bliss.

Vritti-saarupyam itaratra

I/4 The waves are one's identification, otherwise.

> If one remains always identified with the fluctuations of energy, one is identified with the changing world of the seen rather than the stability of the seer.

Five Causes of Action in the Modes of *Chitta*

Vrittayah panchatayyah klishtaklishtah

I/5 Definitions of the waves are fivefold, either obstructing (painful) or non-obstructing.

> All experience of the fluctuations of energy is either painful or non-painful. Pleasure because it is temporary and will end in loss, does not belong to the realm of experience. This is a startling axiom for the person new to yoga. But it is a consistent teaching. Real happiness abides in the seer not the experience of the seen.

Pramaana-viraryaya-vikalpa-nidraa-smritayah

I/6 Evaluation, misperception, conceptualization, sleep, and memory (are the five shapes of the *chitta*).

Pratyaksaanumaanaaganaah pramaanaani

I/7 Direct perception, inference, and testimony are valid means of evaluation.

Viparyayo mithyaajnaanam atad-rupa-pratistham

I/8 Misperception is mistaken knowledge; it is founded on an appearance that is not what is.

Sabda-jnaanaanupati vastu-sunyo vikalpah

I/9 Relying upon a concept in language is conceptualization (fantasy or abstract concept).

Abhava-pratyayaalambana vrittir nidraa

I/10 The arising of thought toward non-wakefulness is sleep.

Anubhuta-visayaasampramosah smritih

I/11 The non-escaping of experienced objects is the act of memory.

Primary Practice

Abhyaasa-vairaagyaabhyaam tan-nirodhah
I/12 Practice and non-attachment are the means of inhibition of *vrittis.*

Tatra sthitau yatno 'bhyaasah
I/13 There, steadiness comes with the practice of vigilance.

Qualities needed for Practice

Sa tu dirgha-kaala-nairantarya-satkaaraasevito dridha-bhumih
I/14 That practice, moreover, needs length of time, without interruption, and devotion to truth to establish in a firm ground.

Dristaanushravika-visaya-vitrishnasya vasikaara-sanjna vairaagyam
I/15 The seen, which is described by others or known as the objects of sensory experience, when not thirsted for brings mastery and the full knowledge of non-attachment.

Tat param purusha-khyaater guna-vaitrishnyam
I/16 That higher non-attachment of identification with the seer, *purusha,* comes when there is no longer a thirsting for the *gunas.*

Lower *Samadhi* Explained as Stages of Inhibition of *Chitta*

Vitarka-vicaaraanandaasmitaa-rupaanugamaat samprajnaatah
I/17 An internal experience of the senses with or without thought, and internal subtle experience with or without internal reflection, a feeling of bliss, a sense of the I-am, these forms of cognitive experience are stages of *nirodha,* the ending of *vrittis.* These stages of inhibition are included within the four stages of *samprajnata samadhi,* or *samadhi* with cognition.

METHOD

The Adult as Learner

When we teach adult yoga students, we appeal to their need to learn and master the difficulties of adult lives. We do not have to inspire them to learn—already they know the value of learning. We inspire them to gain more self-knowledge and self-mastery. We are not expert in their lives. They are the experts, and we are giving them more tools.

The problem of stress
  + Let go of activity and drop into self at the onset of class.

Address day to day need for energy and awareness
  + Between poses pause for self-reflection.

The need for relaxation
  + Let some pauses be real moments of release, relief, repose.

The power of community
  + Facing themselves in silence within a group alleviates the anxiety of isolation.

Tag moments they can use for themselves
  + Make breathing to the center a conscious act.
  + Offer individual poses as ways to approach yoga at home.

The back door to an awareness of energy and consciousness: use of pronouns
  + Use "you, yours" for ownership of their body and emotions.
  + Use "our, ours" for shared activity, moments.
  + Use "the, it" for the detachment of the observer.

TECHNIQUE

Asanas and Their Benefits: Annamayakosha – Inversions, Arm Balances

Inversions - Annamayakosha

> → Encourage deep exhalations of tidal volume that refresh the body.
> → Massage heart and lungs.
> → Strengthen thyroid via pituitary axis.
> → Centralize blood supply in spinal cord and stretch spine.
> → Prevent stagnation of venal blood stagnation in lower limbs, relieving varicose veins.

Balance brahmana and langhana.

Arm Balances - Annamayakosha

> → Build strength, stamina, stability, and flexibility in arm and shoulder musculature.
> → Revitalize nerves and muscles of hands, wrists, and forearms.
> → Peacock combats digestive problems, indigestion, diabetes, constipation, and hemorrhoids.
> → Support health of prostate and pelvic floor.
> → Teach full body awareness via neuro-anatomy of proprioception, and integration with visual, vestibular, and cerebellar functions.

Emphasize brahmana.

Neck, Shoulder and Arm Strengtheners

Standing poses prepare the legs, core and breathing for inversions. To sustain additional weight, further preparation is needed in the upper body with alignment.

Tripod base

explore top of head, align

press head down

pull shoulders to hips

Headstand base

place elbows forearm width

press head down, pull head into hands

press elbows down, pull shoulders to hips

Gliding forearm plank

interlace fingers

with single leg up   *with toes tucked under*

Low side plank   **High side plank**

   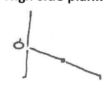

lift hips   *then upper leg and arm*   *depress scapulae*

Down dog preparation

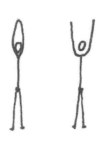

externally rotate upper arms

depress medial scapular spine using lower trapezius

Down dog   **Dolphin**   *deepen the rotation in dolphin*

PRACTICUM

Keep it Simple: Principles of Teaching

1. Be present

What grounds you?

_____

_____

_____

_____

2. Be on time

Arrive early to set the room- lights, fans, music, props

3. Make eye contact… "I see you"

Do you feel comfortable making eye contact with others? Why or why not?

_____

_____

_____

_____

4. Welcome your students

What are some ways a yoga teacher welcomes their students?

_____

_____

_____

_____

5. Make new students a priority

What are some questions to ask a new yoga student?

_____

_____

_____

_____

6. Consider the class size

What are some benefits of a small class?

_____

_____

_____

_____

What are some benefits of a larger class?

_____

_____

_____

_____

7. **When instructing, move slowly around the room to get better angles of vision.**
Catch people doing things right - be sincere with reinforcement (this is part of being 100% present)

8. **Give individual feedback to as many students as possible.**
Be genuine. Don't pretend to have seen a student if you didn't.
   – *I heard...*
   – *I saw...*
   – *I feel...*
   – *I can relate to...*

9. **Try to introduce 1 educational component per class; what is the "take-away?"**
Recall a "lesson" you've learned in yoga:

_____

_____

_____

_____

10. **Be clear.**
Say what you mean, mean what you say

11. **Give 100% of your effort to every single class.**
Show up, even if you don't want to because it's not just about you. Your students are counting on you.

ANATOMY

The Nervous System

We take much for granted when it comes to our movements and volition. What lies underneath it all is a complex feedback system running throughout the body, integrating desires, senses and actions. The nervous system is that central organizing system from vegetative functions to movement, emotion, and thought. It receives, integrates and transmits information based on changes both in the internal and external environments. All sense organs report, are evaluated and then acted upon via the nervous system. In essence, it underlies every action and inaction, and determines our perceptions of mass, speed, volume, time and space.

There are two main divisions – the central nervous system, or CNS, consisting of the brain and spinal cord, and the peripheral nervous system, the nerves that travel throughout the body, innervating organs and muscles. The peripheral system branches off further into these distinctions:

- The sympathetic nervous system, or SNS, aka the "stress response," often referred to as "fight or flight."
- The parasympathetic nervous system, or PNS, which governs the "relaxation response"; often referred to as "rest and digest."

Also refer to Chapter 3, for the nervous system flow chart.

The healthy nervous system is based on an efficient two-way path of communication:

↑ Information <u>coming in</u> to the CNS for processing, traveling along afferent nerves

↓ Commands <u>going out</u> to execute a motor response, traveling along efferent nerves

> **To help remember:**
> *Efferent* = effector, information sent out to bring about an effect
> *Afferent* = 'ad' is Latin for 'to,' carry or "ferry" <u>to</u> the CNS

The Brain
The "triune" brain has these main divisions:
- **Hindbrain.** The lower brain, the oldest evolutionarily speaking, regulates physiology, survival, maintains basic life processes, aka the "reptilian" brain
- **Limbic.** The "middle" brain, the emotional center, manages the "4 Fs" of "fighting, fleeing, fornicating, feeding," [3] aka the "old mammalian" brain
- **Cortex.** The newest evolutionarily, the seat of cognition and creativity, is mostly inhibitory, aka the "new mammalian" brain.

---

[3] This phrase was coined by scientist Robert Ornstein.

The Cerebral Cortex

The **cortex** has four lobes of specialized function. The higher cognitive functions take place in the frontal lobe, including the prefrontal cortex which is known as the center for executive or "top down" functions because it is integral to problem solving, attention and decision making. The frontal lobe also contains the motor cortex, the center of voluntary motor function that is involved in conscious, slow refined movements, as well as Broca's area, where *producing* written and spoken language mostly occurs.

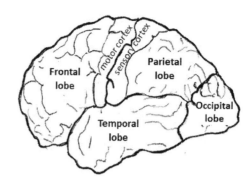

The **parietal** lobe, with its somatosensory cortex, is involved with integrating information from the various senses to help us build a cohesive picture of the world. It aids our sense of spatial relationships and helps in the manipulation of objects and numbers. Lying just below the parietal and frontal lobes is the **temporal** lobe, where our perceptions of sound, smell and sight take place. Wernicke's area is located in the temporal lobe and it is this area that is responsible for the *understanding* of written and spoken language. And, finally, the most posterior portion is the **occipital** lobe, our primary visual area that receives and interprets the projections from the eyes. In between the temporal, parietal and frontal lobes lies the insula, or insular cortex, which is responsible for interoception (sensing the internal state of the body) and regulating homeostasis.

The Midbrain or Limbic System

This area of the brain is the center of emotions, behavior and expression, and includes the amygdala (the "alarm bell" of the stress response), the hippocampus (memory center), the thalamus (a sort of "switching station" that helps filter out unnecessary signals to keep the brain from being overloaded), and the hypothalamus.

The hypothalamus, merely the size of a pea located centrally above the sinus bones, is the control center for autonomic functions. It is involved with a wide range of endocrine and visceral functions, including the regulation of body temperature, water balance, energy resources, feeding behavior, heart rate, breathing rate, and blood pressure. The hypothalamus synthesizes hormones that are released into the pituitary gland for secretion into the blood stream, where they circulate to multiple endocrine glands that regulate autonomic functions of blood pressure, temperature and other visceral actions. The pituitary both stimulates and inhibits the secretion of other glands. This feedback system is dependent upon the circulatory system for conveying information.

Also housed here is an important bundle of nerves called the basal ganglia.[4] The basal ganglia links the thalamus with the motor cortex and orchestrates the body's specific motor responses to sensory stimulation by selecting, in proper sequence and timing, motor neurons that stimulate muscular response. Some motor responses are ready at birth, such as swallowing, and others develop through repetition, such as walking.

Sub-categories of the Basal Ganglia:

Substantia Nigra Interprets and coordinates the sensory information coming from the muscles; assesses and controls changes in lengths of muscles; speed of movement and actual workload. Parkinson's disease is a condition where damage or loss of dopamine in the Substantia Nigra lead to trembling, jerky oscillation while seeking to move.

Globus Pallidus Determines bracing choices; fixation becomes habit and habit becomes character. We need a repertoire of fixations. Most limitations are not "natural."

Striate Body Initiates and monitors stereotyped movements by varying its action with the utility of the movement and the balance needed to accompany the use of the limbs within standard communications. Patterns of sexual arousal, docility, fear, anger, defensiveness all have patterns in striate body. We confuse these patterns of "doing" with identity.

The Hindbrain

The old or lower brain is more reflexive and consists of the brainstem, cerebellum, pons and medulla oblongata. It is made of primitive cephalic[5] ganglia. Here there is a more basic level of sensory integration and motor command. The thalamus, hypothalamus, cerebellum and cortex are offshoots of the older structure, and help with conscious behavior. The old brain is constant within species where relatively fixed responses create the characteristic movements of individual species.

An important area within the brainstem is the **reticular formation**, which can be viewed as a sort of "lower level filter" that helps either to screen out disturbances or enhance and relay relevant information. Most sense organs send information here for processing; otherwise, all sensory input would go directly to the highest centers and create an immediate overload. Because of this filtering task, this is where habituation occurs—constant signals (white noise or constant touch) are ignored. Some additional points to know about the reticular formation...

- Amount of activity corresponds to general levels of mental and physical arousal; for example, when lying down it is calmed, yet stimulated by opening the eyes.

---

[4] Ganglia are bundles of nerve endings, a congregation of synapses and information.
[5] Cephalic means "referring to the head," the center of sensory/motor activity in developing organisms.

- Responsible for sleep/wake cycles.
- Stimulants target the arousal of this area and make us jittery.
- Depressants create lower levels of activity leading to relaxation, grogginess, loss of motor control, as when under anesthesia.
- Artificial overstimulation leads to tetany, stiffening.
- Blocking leads to loss of muscle tone.
- General activity leads to muscle tone, sensory awareness and mental alertness.

The cerebellum is the cauliflower-shaped "little brain" at the back of the cerebral cortex. Although we know the least about the role of the cerebellum, it is involved in more automatic or preprogrammed movement, such as riding a bike. The cerebellum is the main center for integrating proprioceptive information, interpreting sensations related to the body in space and how body parts are related to the whole. It coordinates signals from the inner ears and eyes, keeps balance, and communicates with the cortex to help guide our actions and regulate movement.

Motor connections are both afferent and efferent (in-coming and out-going). They include information from the reticular formation and arousal, the basal ganglia, spinal reflexes and coherent patterns of responding, subthalamus, thalamus, reflex patterns and sequences, and the motor cortex of the cerebrum.

The cerebellum is the center for monitoring and controlling muscular effort in light of the sum of the position and stability within all parts of the body. As in the sensory and motor cortexes where we find the homunculus, the cerebellum has body maps formed by adjacent functions. These maps look less like bodies and more like ink blots. The motor system integrates with other information about the body in the cerebellum as part of its movement. This "quiet" and fast feedback mechanism is what provides integrated, smooth, balanced and appropriate movement. The cerebellum compares "command" with other sensory and motor information including what is gained by the eyes and the vestibular system. Equilibrium is maintained during movement by the semi-circular canals that help us to balance while in motion. Eyes and ears are critical for appropriateness and balance.

The Brain and Meditation

Areas of the brain that have been repeatedly shown to be enhanced by meditation are the prefrontal cortex and the insula. Studies using fMRI scans have demonstrated that long-time meditators have more gray matter in these areas. Also of note are the thalamus and reticular formation. Recall that these two are "filters" (the thalamus a higher level one in the midbrain, and the reticular formation a lower level one in the hindbrain) that help screen out unnecessary or irrelevant sensory signals, an obviously necessary step in the process of meditation.

Meditation has also been proven to increase neurogenesis[6] in the hippocampus, to calm the amygdala, to tell the hypothalamus to stop calling for stress hormones, and to halt overall cortical thinning (age-related brain shrinkage that contributes to cognitive decline).

Anatomy of a Neuron

Neurons are specialized cells of the nervous system. Their function is to receive incoming information from sensory receptors and transmit information to other neurons or effector organs. The dendrites gather information, the cell body integrates that information, and information is sent along the axon out to other neurons. Most axons are covered in fatty myelin sheaths that insulate and speed up the transmission of the signals. The connection is from axon ending to dendrite, yet they are not tethered; there is a gap, or synapse, over which an electrical impulse is translated into a chemical message, called a neurotransmitter. A typical neuron has from 1,000 to 10,000 synapses, thus creating the possibility for coordination of vast amounts of information.

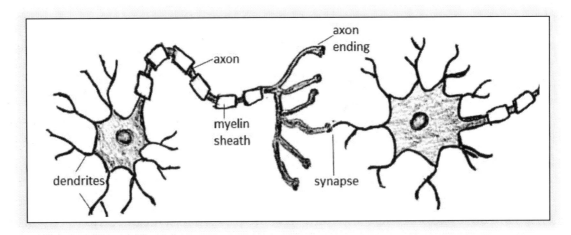

The release of neurotransmitters into the synaptic gap can create palpable changes in mood. The release of dopamine can elevate our mood after exercise or meditation. A lack of dopamine is a possible cause of depression. The release of serotonin brings a feeling of satiation. The natural fluctuations of the release of neurotransmitters and their uptake are part of our experience of the nervous system.

Motor Systems

For the purpose of understanding the relationship of hatha yoga to the nervous system, we will look closely at the motor systems. The motors systems are intimate with sensory systems and perception. Learning and memory are naturally included. Hatha yoga is a learned practice: our increasingly healthy responses to both internal and external

---

[6] Neurogenesis = birth of new neurons.

environments are cultivated by a positive acquisition of behaviors that make us "feel" better.

There are two categories of motors systems: voluntary and involuntary. The voluntary system is what we tend to think of as our motor system. It is responsible for muscular-skeletal activity. The involuntary motor system is largely beyond our conscious control. It is our visceral system made up of the multiple organs that support metabolism, increasing in activity during times of excitation and decreasing during relaxation. Under stress, the autonomic system favors excitation which reduces the maintenance functions of the reproductive, immune and digestive systems. During relaxation, those systems are restored. Hatha yoga brings more conscious control to both motor systems, voluntary and involuntary. During asana we attend to the innate bracing and coordination of movement. During postures and relaxation, attending to the breath regulates autonomic function.

Voluntary Motor System

The action of our muscular-skeletal system depends on the effective input and output of information to the brain. Within the brain we have multiple feedback systems to coordinate the movement, including the thalamus, cerebellum, and information from the eyes and vestibular system in the ears. But our conscious control is perceived and activated in the somatosensory and motor cortices that lie adjacent to one another like a headband across the top of the brain (see figure page 151). Both have a map of the human body that matches the numbers of neurons in each area. The map is in the shape of a little body, the homunculus, with a disproportionately large mouth and hands. This is our conscious sensory input and motor output system. Systemic nerves bring information up the spinal cord to the brain (afferent nerves) and the brain sends information down and out through the spinal cord to the muscles (efferent nerves). Our conscious movement is attended by unconscious spinal reflex arcs that support the chosen action. A movement as simple as lifting an arm requires that we stabilize the opposite side of the torso and hip.

To help us understand how the nervous system creates muscular-skeletal movement, we look at the basics of a muscle. A tendon is a tough band of fibrous connective tissue that usually connects muscles to bones at the ends, while the "belly" of the muscle is the bulging central portion. Each muscle 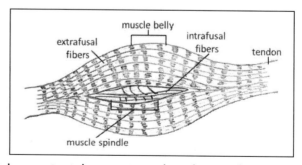 belly contains many muscle spindles, which are stretch receptors that detect change in muscle length and then communicate this information to the CNS. This information is then used by the brain to make fine adjustments and to refine movement. Extrafusal fibers are the outside skeletal fibers that make up the bulk of the muscle. Intrafusal

157

fibers are the inside fibers that make up the muscle spindle and are separated from the rest of the muscle by a collagen sheath.

Our voluntary motor system neurons terminate in motor units in the muscle bellies. When the load increases, more units fire to shorten additional muscle fibers. When one muscle shortens in action (the agonist), the opposing muscle is inhibited (the antagonist) to make room for the action. This reciprocal inhibition means that the nervous system actively inhibits the antagonist so that the agonist can work (refer back to Chapter 3 page 93). This underscores the virtue of inhibition, a primary function of the brain and nervous system. Inhibition creates smooth functioning. As much as 70% of all neurons are inhibitory, promoting discrete activity. Without it, we have crippling instability, restriction, and chaos, seen in such conditions such as Parkinson's disease, schizophrenia, and epilepsy.

Involuntary Motor System
Our visceral activity relies upon the involuntary motor system. Healthy physiology is called homeostasis. It is a fluctuating system of arousal, relaxation and digestion. The fluctuations of arousal and relaxation are broadly tied to fundamental sleep/wake cycles but are no less related with mental functioning. Perceived threat leads to sympathetic arousal, the endemic core of health concerns in our modern lifestyle. The shared stressors of schedules, traffic, technology, world events and pollutants, without adding the personal stresses of loss, divorce, and relocation, all challenge our physiology. The value and success of yoga is largely the benefit of increasing mental stamina in the face of challenge so that under duress the body retains balance and does not precipitate toward illness.

Our physiology is linked with our limbic system, the emotional brain. When we are angry or fearful, a small ganglion called the amygdala fires sympathetic neurons and creates global arousal. During arousal, the nervous system has a potent relationship with the endocrine system to sustain increased energy. The powerful steroid of cortisol is released by the adrenal glands into the blood stream. Sympathetically, the thyroid gland raises the heat of metabolism. Success in combatting stress is followed by parasympathetic relaxation, which restores homeostasis by removing the "stress" hormones from the blood stream, allowing the digestive, reproductive and immune systems to restore to normal levels. Lack of success creates a brittle systemic environment, making us vulnerable to illness, disease, and auto-immune conditions. Yoga and meditation develop mental stamina and resilience in the face of environmental stressors. Research on the brain indicates that with a meditation practice, the pre-frontal cortex, the part of the brain that modulates our emotional responses, thickens. Thickening indicates that decision-making is active and can regulate emotion, inhibiting the amygdala's response to stress.

The Voluntary Motor System In-Depth [7]

The voluntary system is at our command. We move as we see fit -- looking, reaching, grasping, and lifting with striated muscle organized to stir our skeletal frame. Our striated muscles receive our conscious commands. They also sense as they move, giving us important information about mass and speed, bracing and balancing so that our movement is

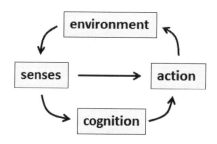

smooth and effective. Yet we have unconscious reflex systems in place to stabilize our movement, and feedback systems to assess inner and outer tensions and challenges. Thus, one-third of this voluntary motor system is unconscious, stabilizing and refining our conscious action.

Conscious & Unconscious Elements within the Voluntary Motor System[8]
The alpha system is our conscious system of movement made up of large nerve fibers[9] going from the cortex to skeletal muscle. The nerves end in a striated muscle where the

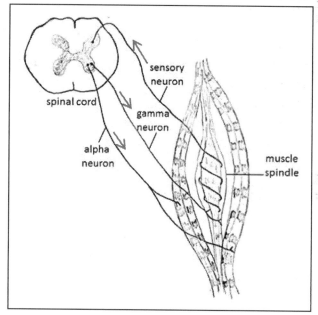

fibers are lined up to work as a group. A sensory neuron wraps around the muscle spindle in a spiral pattern and is called an annulospiral receptor.[10] It detects change by lengthening and shortening as skeletal muscle fibers around it lengthen and shorten. Movement and sensation are closest here. The spindles are motor units that feel their own action and send messages to the spine.

In the spine, a sensory neuron synapses with a motor neuron and forms a reflex arc. The simplest control of our movement is the "myotatic stretch reflex," where a sudden change in length of a muscle spindle triggers a contraction of the same muscle, which in turn stimulates other skeletal muscles to join and assist. This basic reflex maintains the length of the muscle and therefore posture. It is a valuable protective mechanism to prevent unexpected stretching. Think of jumping

---

[7] The Involuntary Motor System is covered in detail in "Chapter 7 Breathing."
[8] This view of the motor systems is based on "Muscle as Sense Organ," chapter 8 of Job's Body, Deanne Juhan, Station Hill Press, 1987.
[9] A nerve fiber is an axon covered by a fatty myelin sheath. The long axon grows from the nerve body that has dendrites of hair-like fibers that act as the receiving end of the nerve.
[10] There are also secondary sensory neurons called "flower spray." Annulospiral are primary.

off of a high platform – the muscles in the legs contract rapidly to minimize the possibility of injuring joints and ligaments.

This reflex arc is part of our gamma, or unconscious, motor response. The gamma system is composed of smaller nerve fibers that go from intrafusal spindles to ganglia in the lower brain. Intrafusal spindles lie between the annulospiral receptor embedded in the belly of the muscle and the tendon. The alpha and gamma systems are linked by the annulospiral receptors that synapse in the spinal column with alpha partners. That is, the intrafusal fiber stimulates the alpha system via the basic annulospiral spindle. One third of all neurons are gamma, or unconscious.

Two systems of motor nerves, conscious and unconscious...

Alpha (Conscious)	Cerebral/ cortical control	Extrafusal (main/outer)	Large diameter nerve fibers, the majority of our motor neurons	Moves skeletal muscles through contraction
Gamma (Unconscious)	Lower brain/ spinal cord	Intrafusal (inner, found in muscle spindle)	Smaller diameter nerve fibers; also smaller in number (1/2 as many as alpha motor neurons)	Tracks & refines movement; adjusts sensitivity to muscle length; reflexes

Golgi Tendon Organs (GTO)

Golgi tendon organs are part of the unconscious gamma system and they detect the load on the muscle. The receptors lie among the collagen bundles in the tendons and have a zig-zag shape that detects change. Each is responsive to about 10-12 alpha motor units. The GTO is a gauge of the force of muscle pulling on the bone. The GTO assesses the exact resistance that is overcome to create an action, by measuring distance within a given time.

A lengthened muscle is weaker. In a lengthened position there is less overlap of the fibers within the muscle belly where contraction takes place. A longer muscle will feel more resistance. Fatigue or mood can shift the feeling of resistance. In yoga practice, we use muscles in their lengthened position to educate the GTO's to not release under the load of more resistance. In this way, the lengthened shape is stronger, a definition of flexibility.

Our experience of the mass of an object is measured by the sensory impressions of both tendon and muscle receptors. Together they assess mass: the measure of resistance to movement.

Golgi Reflex Arc

The Golgi reflex arc is sometimes referred to as the "inverse myotatic reflex" because instead of providing a muscular contraction and bracing action, it tells the muscle to release in order to prevent tendon injury. It is a link between sensory and motor functions. The GTO synapses with motor neurons within the spinal cord that also are activated by the alpha system. However, the GTO synapses with an inhibitory motor nerve to prevent damage to tendons and bones. The power to inhibit alpha neurons is power to protect, and higher brain influences are present.

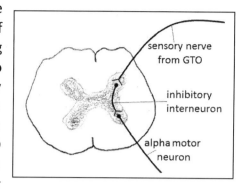

sensory nerve from GTO

inhibitory interneuron

alpha motor neuron

With GTO feedback, muscles adjust to apply the appropriate effort for any job, especially essential for fine motor adjustments given variables of fatigue, body position, excitement, boredom, and mood. The tension of a muscle needs a wide range of adjustments and rapid shifts. The higher brain, the conscious voluntary system from the sensory/motor cortex can control "required tension." Sensory/motor adjustments are the most intimate feedback adjustments in the body. Movement leads to immediate sensory shifts that adjust movement. And the gamma system is entirely unconscious.

The Value of the Gamma System – Reflexes

Simple reflex – "myotatic stretch reflex"
- The annulospiral receptor synapses with the motor unit of a corresponding alpha neuron, and when stimulated by a sudden stretch applied by an external force, initiates movement. Net effect is to oppose the stretching force and maintain the current length of the muscle.
- Shifting position and weight of limbs initiates the reflex.
- "Static" stretch reflex is steady.
- "Dynamic" stretch reflex is sudden.
- Resting tension—the higher the resting tension the more violent the reflex.
- Higher brain centers set the tension value.
- External forces tug from outside, and internal moods, etc, tug from inside.
- Stress and anxiety drive up the resting tension.
- The stretch reflex can become a mental and physical defense mechanism.
- Bodywork and yoga postures provide slow, patient, unthreatening pressure and stretches that initiate cycles of trust and surrender, and calm the mental turmoil.

The withdrawal reflex is more complex
Sharp pain leads to shock and jerk.
- Higher brain attitudes about pain and relative anxiety modulate the response.
- Otherwise, pain leads to contraction leads to increasing pain.
- Bullying a sore area leads to more stretch and withdrawal reflexes.

Withdrawal when flexors of affected limb contract
Crossed-extensor reflex:
- Extend opposite limb to push whole body away from source of pain.
- With intense pain, whole body twists, jumps, ducks and cringes.
- Habit of over-correction leads to distortion and a large amount of energy is wasted.

Learned reflexes
- Learned means that we move beyond reflexes that assist us with respect to gravity & pain (bracing and avoidance) and preservation of life; we develop reflexes to direct and enrich life.
- Two earliest reflexes:
  - Prenatal, the head turns away when the cheek is stroked.
  - Postnatal, the head turns toward.

Danger becomes nourishment
- Two basic responses are polar opposites; withdraw and avoid versus extend and explore. In yoga, we pursue appropriate movement that results in pleasure because we avoid pain. Otherwise, we could live with a low pain threshold that triggers discomfort and pain more often. Our positive response to life is to extend, explore and learn, while becoming neutral with discomfort that might normally be felt as pain.

Conditioned reflexes
Conditioned reflexes are new patterns of motor learning dominated by feeling, that is, sensory information to the higher brain. Changes in feeling can radically shift defensive postures. With positive tactile experiences, new emotional and intellectual associations develop, leading to wider choices rather than defended positions. New conditioned responses supported by new sensations and facilitated by new attitudes mean that the reflex of extension and opening can be reinforced.

Alpha-Gamma Integration
The gamma system will follow the lead of the alpha if alpha movement corresponds to expected norms of the gamma system. Or the gamma system can initiate movement via the gamma loop. The gamma loop:
- Gamma motor neurons are stimulated by intrafusal fibers that lie near the annulospiral gauges in the muscle belly.
- They fire the spinal reflex arc.
- The alpha is stimulated to mimic the initiative of the gamma and the annulospiral is quieted.

When there is stress or injury, the alpha-gamma integration gets out of balance and the result is a muscle spasm. As the muscle fully contracts, the muscle spindle gets reset back into a state of balance.

Space and Time
- As with mass, time and space are measured by our motor systems.
- Time: alpha system is duration of neural bursts.
- Space: gamma system is the starting and stopping of lengths of muscle fibers measured by annulospiral gauges.

Proprioception

Proper, efficient movement relies on having a good "starting point." Proprioception, sometimes referred to as our "6th sense," provides this sense of the relative position of the body. It is what allows us to move about in the dark, to type, to paint without looking at the brush, and to walk without constantly looking at our feet. If all of our actions required constant vision and cognition, it would be extremely tiring.

Proprioception relies on information from three basic areas—receptors in muscle spindles and joints provide information on what part of the body has moved, how fast, and with how much force; sensory neurons from the inner ear (vestibular sense) detect motion and orientation; and, mechanoreceptors on the skin and fingers add valuable input on pressure, vibration and temperature. All of this goes to the brain to be integrated as perception.

There are also unconscious and conscious aspects of proprioception. An example of conscious proprioception is posture, and this takes place in the cortex and spine; whereas balance and reflexes are mostly unconscious and occur more in the cerebellum (hindbrain). In yoga, proprioception is called body awareness. It is a touch system, sensitive to sound and speech, and sensitive to our mental states.

Learning New Patterns

Muscle Tone

Spindles and GTO's control excitation and inhibition and keep our muscles in a narrow range of tension that shifts with various tasks. Basic tone holds the skeleton together and maintains structural integrity, respiration, posture, bracing as we move. Shifting background tone gives a stable and flexible framework. From birth: firm structure, posture, respiratory rhythms, swallowing and eliminating, grasping, withdrawing, and tracking with the eyes are already developed.

Getting a "Feel" for it

The sensory roles of the annulospiral receptor and the Golgi tendon organ are the keys for adjusting tone and establishing a "feel" for length and tension. The "feel" is maintained by the gamma motor system, the reflex arcs and the alpha skeletal muscles. All muscles are "felt" by the mind as they work whether consciously or not. Muscular feeling is supplying the nervous system with constant sensory information so that we combine free motion with basic structural stability. The exquisite sophistication of the system is guided by sensory cues.

Acquiring Reflexes

Repetition leads to learned reflexes. When we gain a "feel" for something, it becomes like a reflex. Experimentation leads to a conservative norm. We drop from one level to another in the brain; conscious mind or sensory/motor cortex gives way to the brain stem. Humans need to acquire many reflexes, which happens through trial and error. Individual stereotypes and characteristics come forth as learned patterns dominate and limitations become habit. A reflex develops as an event becomes a tendency, which becomes a habit and finally a personal identity. Gestures lead to postures that become personal identity. Yoga is clearly a method for adjusting reflexes to resonate with healthy patterns of movement and mental ease.

Tone and Mental State

A stable posture alters with the environment and mental states. A "sense of effort" is both mental and physical. Consider the difference between walking up a hill while happy, versus while depressed. Effort varies.

Best of Two Worlds

The gamma system of the basal ganglia is conservative. Its value lies in establishing tonus and species constant behavior. The alpha system of the cerebral motor cortex is experimental and modifies reflexes to suit situations. Bad habits can be ingrained quickly. Bodywork and yoga postures elicit valuable sensations and feeling so that possibilities for movement and shifts in identity can be awakened.

Effort

As we apply effort, the distinction between sensory and motor functions is not clear. We gauge effort, which requires information as we act. The "sense of effort" is a special sense. Mass and weight are measured by the effort needed to resist gravity.

Physiological effort includes basic tone and weight of the body which change with attitudes and interests. We also need more force with a heavier object and more stasis with a heavier body. There can be a "tyranny of the normal" in an effort to maintain our weight. Tension can lead to compressions and more fuel is needed to maintain "normal," which leads to depletion of energy. Depletion means an increase in waste from metabolism, and a decrease in circulation adding to discomfort and dysfunction. Bodywork and yoga postures alleviate excessive effort. Precision of effort means appropriate effort and ease.

Yoga Postures and Meditation

In the practice of asana, the weight and tension of the body and the force of gravity provide resistance. Working effectively with resistance is what enhances our awareness of movement and the power of our conscious control of our actions. Push and pull, the paired actions of agonist and the recruited antagonist, appropriate work for an action, the overall "felt" value of alignment and the incessant use of repetition and staying to refine posture, all train the nervous system to healthy patterns of movement and mental ease.

Asana practice teaches the virtues of support of stable structure and extension into new ways of being. We develop respect for the unconscious refinement and the ways our nervous system supports learning. We value the natural vegetative functions and develop more awareness of how we respond to stressors and alleviate our response. We replace unhealthy patterns with new ones, always looking for possibility, as we create new levels of stability.

In meditation, the benefits are deepened. From the position of the seer we can see our mental state, which brings about real change in the body. Without reducing mental impressions and tendencies, we remain in a position of changing identities rather than seeing through identities that inhibit appropriate choices and responses. Meditation takes our asana practice deeper. Rather than depending on our biological systems to brace and balance us, we reach toward the unwavering experience of consciousness to find stability.

Summary of the Nervous System in terms of the koshas

Body: Brahmana/langhana (heating/cooling) balance of sympathetic and parasympathetic divisions of the autonomic nervous system quiets emotion.

Senses: Focusing on breathing quiets cognitive senses and allows for more proprioception (body awareness). The narrowing arena of senses creates disinterest, attentiveness, and a restful condition in the nervous system.

Mind: Shifts to learning, a higher order function. We are creating new neuronal pathways. The possessive nature of the mind is minimized.

Ego: Our agency is lessened. We observe more, keeping our attention on the limited sphere of the body and breath, the more vegetative functions of survival.

Intellect: We keep the intellect active with refined choices, including breath awareness and awareness of consciousness.

Consciousness is a higher order, integrative brain function.

ASSIMILATION

Content

Samkhya sutras:
➤ List the five sources of knowledge and the five causes of action.

➤ Describe the movement of nutation.
- – Sacral movement:

- – Ilial movement:

- – Ischial movement:

➤ And counter-nutation.
- – Sacral movement:

- – Ilial movement:

- – Ischial movement:

Contemplation

➤ Practice and detachment – which comes first?

➤ Contemplate both: does detachment help practice?

➤ Does practice help with healthy detachment?

➤ Do inversions help us with our inner practices? How?

Practice

➤ Do preparation for inversion poses even if you already do inversions.

➤ Practice a standing series with awareness of length, load and timing.

➤ End with deep relaxation.

➤ Then sit for meditation.

Poses

➤ Draw a series of poses that include Hip ROM

Yoga is not for him who over-eats, nor for him who fasts excessively;
not for him, O Arjuna, who sleeps too much,
nor for him who stays awake long.
Bhagavad Gita 6/16

Chapter Seven – Breathing

SS 10 The Five Winds
Revisit Poses papers: adding more elements of breathing
Continue with the Value of Yoga Paper

The story of the seventh chapter: breath and mind move together. Breathing well tempers the mind and creates homeostasis in the body. Homeostasis is the basis of somatic and systemic health: a closer look at the involuntary nervous system, the endocrine system and the power of breath to create balance.

Contents

Bless the fingers,
For they are as darting as fire.
Bless the little hairs of the body,
For they are softer than grass.
Mary Oliver

PHILOSOPHY

Samkya Sutra 10: The Five Winds

This air is like honey for all beings
and all beings are honey for this air

This shining immortal person who is in this air
and this shining immortal breath in the body
is just this Self, just this Brahman, and this is all

This space is like honey for all beings
and all beings are honey for this space

This shining immortal person who is in this space
and this shining immortal space in the body
is just this Self, just this Brahman, and this is all

This shining immortal truth is honey for all beings
and all beings are honey for this truth

This shining immortal person who is this truth
and this shining immortal truth in the body
is just this Self, just this Brahman, and this is all

He who dwells in the air
yet is within the air

whom the air does not know
whose body the air is

who controls the air from within
he is your Self
the inner controller
the immortal

"Brhad-aaranyaka Upanisad"
Madhu-vidya (honey doctrine) & seventh Brahmana

Breath and thought are twins. After presenting the five sources of action as the differing modes of the intellect, Kapil presents breath as the power to act in congruence with thought. These not only refer to the life breath but also the movement of life energy in the body: upward, downward, in the center, spreading throughout, and in the head. In the Yoga system these are collectively known as *prana*, although the first, the upward movement, is also called *prana*. The other four are *apana, samana, vyana*, and *udana*. These five main movements of energy support all vital functions of the body; with our vitality we bring thought into speech and action.

The Five Vayus:
Prana, Apana, Samana, Vyana, Udana

Prana	upward moving	governs lungs, heart, hands
Apana	downward moving	governs large intestine, elimination, reproduction, legs
Samana	central	governs digestion
Vyana	spreading energy	governs circulation, touch
Udana	head	governs brain, senses, thyroid gland & above

The *vayus* and the *doshas* can be correlated. The *pita dosha* is related with the heat of digestion and breath in the upper diaphragm. The *pitta dosha* benefits from the spreading energy of *vyana vayu*. The *vata dosha* favors the ideas and inspiration of *udana vayu*, but the "seat" of *vata* is in *kapha*. This means that without the balance of *apana vaya*, there would be little balance in the system. Similarly, the "seat" of *kapha* is in *vata*. The *kapha dosha* finds balance through the stimulation of upward movement of *prana* and the inspiration of ideas.

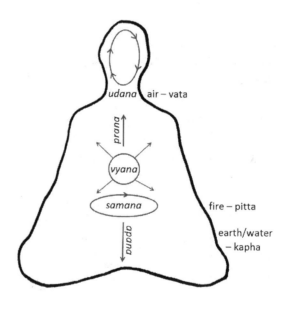

Pranayama

Pranayama means extension of breath. *Prana* means both breath and life energy. *Ayama* means to extend or lengthen. To extend one's breath means to lengthen the time of each breath and, by extension, one's lifespan. *Pranayama* includes vigilance, awareness, and mastery of our breath and life energy.

The correlation of breath with life energy is intuitively obvious since if we cease to breathe we cease to live. More specifically, our breath indicates how we are using our life energy. For instance when we are anxious, we engage in thoracic breathing. Yogic science has noted the varying states of breath that correspond with varying states of

171

mind and body and has developed practices for manipulating the breath in order to affect physiological change and a simultaneous change in perception.

The practices of *pranayama* enliven the system and bring fresh oxygen and relief from the lethargy of *tamoguna*. The practices also calm the restlessness of *rajoguna*. The balance between liveliness and calm increases the values of *sattoguna,* mental clarity, lightness, and ease. The restfully alert state reduces the power of impressions and tendencies,[1] alleviating the pull of the conditioning in the nervous system. Impressions and tendencies are held in the *chitta.* They can be useful or harmful. A calm state leaves room for conscious choice, freeing us to respond and not react. The calm state reduces desire and doubt,[2] so we feel less confusion and misery that come from seeking to fulfill endless cravings and desires.

There is a relationship between *prana* and the chakras. The chakras are energy centers that, according to the teachings of yoga, mediate our relationship with the environment.[3] We are in relationship with subtle energy and the gross material world on the five levels of the *tanmatras*, the principles of sound, touch, sight, taste and smell. These are correlated with the five elements of earth, water, fire, air and space, the neuro-endocrine system and the five lower chakras from the base of the pelvis to the throat. Our ability to increase the vitality of the body and the focus of the mind is because of the stimulation of these centers. The potential energy of the chakras is available for internal homeostasis and action, and can be amplified through *pranayama* as means of approaching the goal of yoga, which is to create a stable and powerful flow of energy in the body that supports higher states of consciousness.

Types of breathing exercises related with the 3 gunas:

Rajas	Heating – arousal	Related with backbends
Tamas	Cooling – relaxation	Related with forward folds
Sattva	Balancing via both nostrils	

Examples of *Pranayama*:

Heating	Bastrika	Breath of fire, inhaling and exhaling with force like a bellows
Cooling	Sitali	Inhaling through both nostrils, and exhaling through the mouth while curling the tongue like a tube
Balancing	Nadi shodhana	Alternate nostril breathing

---

[1] Impressions are called *samskara,* and tendencies are *vasana. Samskara & vasana,* held in the *chitta,* follow us through lifetimes. Practice purifies the *chitta* of impressions based in wrong knowledge and fanciful thinking.

[2] Doubt, *vikalpa,* is a vacillating uncertain state, and *samkalpa* is the planning stage of action. *Kama* is more simply desire.

[3] Review Section I/3 "The Chakra System."

The *bandhas*[4] are necessary for containment of the *prana*. The stimulating effect of many *pranayama* practices (*rajas*) is balanced by the containment of the *bandhas* (*tamas*), leading to balance (*sattva*)[5].

Specificity of *Pranayama*

The power of *pranayama* lies in our ability to use breath appropriately. As with *asana*, *pranayama* addresses specific conditions. If there is a predominance of fire or *pitta* in the body, a cooling or balancing breath would be appropriate. If there is predominance of earth/water or *kapha*, a heating breath is appropriate. If there is a predominance of *vatta,* the most appropriate breath is a complete breath that balances all the *doshas*.

Doshas, Emotions, and the Balancing Effects of *Pranayama*

The *doshas* of *vata, pitta* and *kapha* can be correlated with the power of emotions that run through the body. The positive grounding influence of *kapha* assists us to feel fear and to handle the emotion. The positive energetic experience of *pitta* helps us to feel anger and effectively express it by establishing healthy boundaries. The positive power of *vata* allows us to release the grip of our grief and dissolve back toward homeostasis.

An imbalance in *kapha* increases the value of fear to grip or freeze the other emotions. Fear will inhibit all *prana* and all emotion. An imbalance in *pitta* encourages a lack of inhibition of emotion and inappropriate displays of feeling. An imbalance in *vata* stimulates confusion, dissipation of energy, and an inability to recognize emotion.

The practices of *pranayama,* because they quiet the mind and balance the body, activate the ability to witness emotion without needing to change the environment. This allows us to understand emotion as information and to respond appropriately to our environment.[6]

General Benefits of *Pranayama* Practice[7]

Pranayama is a practice that increases vitality and the concurrent awareness of how we spend that energy. The benefit of *pranayama* practice is a subjective increase in energy and vitality and an increase in clarity of mind, that is, a calm, alert mind. Using an analogy from Physics, *pranayama* increases our "potential" energy (resting), and because of a simultaneous increase in awareness, creates an awareness of how we use our "kinetic" energy (acting). To use another analogy, *pranayama* puts money in the bank. Once we have a full bank account, we become more conscious of our spending. If we never have quite enough, we spend before we can save, or withdraw more than we have.

---

[4] The three *bandhas* are holds in the root, abdomen, and chin that modify the movement of the five *pranas*.
[5] Refer back to Chapter 3 for a review on the *gunas* and *doshas*.
[6] *Pranayama* practices are covered in the Technique section: Teaching *Pranayama*.
[7] Further discussion of physiological benefits of *pranayama* is in the Anatomy section: Lungs and Heart.

When mind is subtle, breath is subtle; when mind is unified, it moves energy.
When breath is subtle, mind is subtle; when energy is unified, it moves mind.
First we develop energy then we can stabilize the mind, because the mind alone
has no set place to work upon. So focus energy as a starting point.
From working with energy comes the preservation of pure energy.
Secret of the Golden Flower

TECHNIQUE

Teaching Pranayama

When we practice *pranayama* we are moving the five winds of *prana, apana, samana, vyana,* and *udhana.* They are activated to enhance the health of the physical body. An increase in vitality, equanimity, and clarity of mind develop from appropriate practice. *Pranayama* is best taught gradually along with *hatha* practices that open the breathing apparatus.

Right and Left Nostrils
In yoga, the right and left nostrils are correlated with the autonomic nervous system. Within the word *"hatha"* of *hatha* yoga, *"ha"* means sun, and *"tha"* means moon. The right nostril is related with the arousal of the sympathetic division. The left nostril is related with the relaxation of the parasympathetic division. Thus the *pranayama* called *surya* (sun) *bedana* heats the body by amplifying the breath in the right nostril. Similarly, *chandra* (moon) *bedana* cools the body by amplifying the energy of the left nostril. *Nadi shodhana,* alternate nostril breathing, balances the two sides and is useful for calming and energizing at the same time. *Nadi shodhana* is a safe beginning practice, after first learning the complete three-part breath.

Types of *Pranayama*

Beginner	
Complete breath	Balances all *doshas*, all *pranas*
Ujjayi – ocean breath	Narrowing the throat creates sustained, conscious breathing balancing all *pranas*
Nadi shodhana	Alternate nostril, lengthens the breath balances *prana* & *apana, ha* & *tha*
Surya (sun – *ha*) *bedhana*	Right to left nostril, stimulates *prana*
Chandra (moon – *tha*) *bedhana*	Left to right nostril, stimulates *apana*

Intermediate	
Bastrika – bellows breath	Pumping the abdomen activates *pitta,* assists *kapha,* helps *vyana prana*
Kapalabhati – shining skull	Forced exhalation from the diaphragm that clears sinuses and activates *udana* energy in the head
"Breath of Joy" *Bastrika & Krama*	Combines *bhastrika & krama* *Bastrika* – a vigorous abdominal exhalation while coming forward *Krama*[1] – three gradual inhalations that lead to a deep exhalation called *anuloma krama*[1] and generally not done with *bastrika.*

Advanced	
Breath ratios and rounds: Initially in/out 1:1	Increase ratios gradually; extending beyond can irritate the nervous system. *dirga* – long and steady *sukshma* – smooth and subtle
Add retention & suspension ratio To teach retention &suspension	1:1:1:1, in/retain/out/suspend. continue with 2:1:2:1, 3:1:3:1.

By use of ratios, *pranayama* practice lengthens the exhalation, *puraka*; lengthens the inhalation, *rechaka*; and lengthens the suspension or retention, *kumbhakam*. Exhaling and holding out is called *bahya kumbhakam*. Inhaling and holding in is called *antar kumbhakam*.

Ways to Explore the Teaching of Breathing
Always practice alone before you teach in a group.

Deep breathing during the poses
- → Lower lobes of lungs fill with abdominal breath
- → Middle lobes of lungs with thoraco-diaphragmatic breath
- → Upper lobes of lungs with collar bones, and thus arms, lifted
- → During deep breathing, holding the back and upper chest firm resists the opening of diaphragm, thereby deepening the breath.

Square breath
- → While seated or lying down
- → Breath ratio 2:2:2:2 (inhale/retain/exhale/suspend)

Alternate nostril breath
- → While seated
- → Breath ratio 1:1 (inhale and exhale equal), increasing to 1:2

→ Add retention and suspension ratio 1:1:1 (in/retain/out)
→ Gradually lengthen the exhale to 1:1:2 (in/retain/out)
→ Gradually lengthen the retention to 1:2:2 (in/retain/out)

Vigorous breathing
→ Gradually teach vigorous breathing with movement during the poses
→ Vigorous breathing increases overall *prana* and this energy is contained with the *bandhas*.

The *Bandhas*

Bandha means "lock" or "hold." A *bandha* creates energetic containment using physical muscles in precise places in the body. Please only teach if you practice them.

- First teach *uddiyana bandha* (abdominal) for a massage and cleansing value with *bahya kumbhakam*, the lungs empty. Also teach in a milder form to assist forward folds, and to find abdominal support during most postures.

- Secondly, explore *mula bandha* (root) within the poses, especially forward folds and downward-facing dog pose. Bring the awareness into standing poses.

- Thirdly, *jalandhara bandha* (chin) is taught gradually to help lengthen the upper spine and to open the energy into the head, *udana prana*.

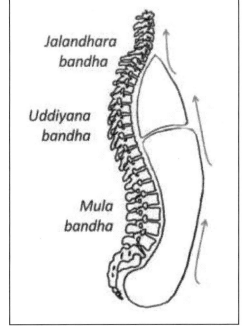

- The *bandhas,* when released, stimulate the flow of *prana* within the healthy containment of the body. The *bandhas* are an advanced teaching and considered essential for an effective and healthy practice. If you teach vigorous breathing, the abdominal hold is necessary. Look for how the root hold is engaged in the seated and standing *asanas* so you can begin to highlight the muscle groups involved in the root hold during *pranayama* practice. *Mula bandha* and *jalandhara bandha* are essential for inhaling and retaining the breath, *antar kumbakam*.

Asanas and Their Benefits: Pranamayakosha

Forward Folds - Pranamayakosha

→ Invigorate *apana vayu* that nourishes *prana*, the upward flow.
→ Bring greater concentration of *prana* to neck, upper back, and throat
→ *Samana* and *udana vayus* activated in child, rabbit and *yoga mudra*.
→ Refresh and stimulate.

Twists - Pranamayakosha

→ Activate samana and prana vayus.
→ Revitalize

Lateral Bends - Pranamayakosha

→ Open *samana vayu* centered in abdomen and radiating out like a star.
→ Some *vyana vayu* moving *prana* from core to upper and lower extremities.
→ Amplify breathing.

Hip ROM - Pranamayakosha

→ Open *apana vayu* below navel that can be released toward upward flow of *prana*.
→ Bring a feeling of safety, quieting mind and emotions.

Standing Poses - Pranamayakosha

→ Mountain pose opens *prana* and *apana vayu*.
→ Triangle balances all five *vayus*.
→ With a rotated spine, *samana vayu* is activated.
→ Build a wakeful stamina and confidence.

Standing Balances - Pranamayakosha

→ Emphasize *samana vayu*, helping with digestive fire.
→ Helpful for *prana, vyana,* and *apana vayus*.
→ Develop mental poise and a single-minded focus for meditation.

Backbends - Pranamayakosha

→ Stimulate *samana vayu*, with *prana, vyana,* and *udana*.
→ Chakrasana (wheel) activates all *vayus*.
→ Increase energy, vigor, and youthful vitality.
→ Help regulate moods and emotions.
→ Relieve stress response and mental agitation.
→ Strengthen concentration and determination.

Inversions - Pranamayakosha
→ Activate *prana vayu*, upward movement into heart and lungs, → Activate *udana*, in throat and head, → Activate *apana* and *samana* for digestion. → Alleviate depression and insomnia. → Enhance physical and mental relaxation.

Arm balances - Pranamayakosha
→ Activate *samana vayu*. → Develop power of concentration and determination.

PRACTICUM

Keep it Simple: Implementing Energy Flow and Vinyasa

Implementing Energy Flow in the Body

- Movements and rhythm is slow enough to follow breath
- Breath is easy; Sound is soft. Texture is smooth.
- Excessive effort is avoided. Ease is found in every pose.
- Be aware of habitual reactions to discomfort in a pose and minimize unnecessary/unrelated contractions
  - Wiggle Fingers
  - Soften jaw
- Alignment is attained through knowledge of the pose coupled with intuitive response and surrender
- Encourage softness before and during stretching. Then, slowly go deeper as tension releases
- Slow, mindful transitions paired with breath

Implementing Vinyasa When Teaching

- Breathe with the class
- Encourage effort and ease
  - Effort = Setting the pose up, Attention to alignment, Focus
  - Ease = breath awareness
- Cue early
- Say the pose, then the breath
- Each movement and pose sets up the next movement and pose
- Before flowing through postures that will be repeated, allow time in the posture in order to create muscle memory and ease later
- Remember to cue breath even when postures are held longer
  - What is happening on the inhale?
  - What is happening on the exhale?

ANATOMY

The Involuntary Motor System

Physiology and Homeostasis

Homeostasis is a term used to describe a state of physiological balance in our internal environment. This state is achieved by the autonomic division of the central nervous system. The term homeostasis was first coined by Walter B. Cannon in 1929 to describe a complex set of biological processes that maintain balance in the body. There are many variables in the body that fluctuate within narrow limits. When limits are reached, the body will trigger autonomic mechanisms, such as those for breathing rates to maintain proper O_2 and CO_2 concentrations, for temperature control, or for a behavioral response as in the case of hunger or thirst. SNS (sympathetic nervous system) responses shift us away from homeostasis so we are able to do what is necessary for survival. However, with sustained stress, homeostasis can be difficult to maintain.

Stress
The word "stress" is a term from Physics meaning, "the applied force or system of forces that tends to strain or deform a body, measured by the force acting per unit area."[8] The term is used in the field of engineering, and was borrowed from engineering and applied to our human experience by Hungarian endocrinologist, Hans Seyle.[9] When we say, "I am stressed out," we mean that the forces acting upon us are causing a "strain" or "deformity" (problems).

The Stress Response
The "stress response" is the response of our nervous system to the "stress" of the environment. Difficulties arise when we cannot quiet the stress response. The stress of the environment can never be completely stopped, though it can be reduced. The core of Hans Seyle's theory is that our stress response is adaptive. If a predator is within one's view, it is adaptive to run or fight. Thus Seyle borrowed the term, "the fight or flight" response, which was coined by Walter B. Cannon.[10] Provided we succeed, we know there will be other predators, both literally and figuratively. Seyle defined four stages of the stress response as follows:

1. Alarm – SNS turns "all on"
2. Resistance – the body attempts to return us to homeostasis
3. Exhaustion- if the alarm continues, efforts at resistance deplete us
4. Death – assuming no conscious control, the organism dies

---

[8] "Stress" definition 5. American Heritage Encyclopedia Dictionary.
[9] *The Stress of Life*, Hans Seyle.
[10] *Bodily Changes in Pain, Hunger, Fear, and Rage*, W.B. Cannon; Appleton, N.Y, 1929.

If we are a good fighter we might enjoy the prospect of a good fight. This is called "stress hardiness."[11] The attitude that helps us deal with stress is optimism. What has been found through research is that perceiving stress as a challenge, rather than a threat, diminishes the adverse effects of the stress response on the body. Problems arise with the stress of life only when we cannot turn off the systems in the body that initiate fight or flight and the sustained energy necessary for survival. When the stress response is initiated by the autonomic nervous system, it also initiates a reduction in the function of other systems of the body needed for healthy maintenance that are not needed during moments of "fight or flight," such as the immune system, the reproductive system, and the digestive system. The survival of the body is favored over the maintenance of the body and continuation of the species.

Optimum functioning of the "fight or flight" response means that the system activates and then de-activates. When we watch the perceived stressors diminish on the horizon, we relax. And we learn to stay calmer when they come herding back. In times of discomfort, it is adaptive to minimize the "fight or flight" response and habituate the nervous system to remain calm.

Illness is caused by excess or depletion, exaggerated response or under-reaction, and the compensation of our bodies by establishing set points that are not in balance. The secretion of too much insulin causes hypoglycemia. Too little causes diabetes. Hypertension comes with elevated blood pressure. Dizziness and fatigue come with lowered blood pressure (hypotension). Dizziness is a way for the body to suspend activity while the blood pressure adjusts. Given the opportunity, the body will seek a healthy homeostasis.

Hans Seyle noted that those people suffering from "stress" as perceived threat did not return to normal homeostasis in the autonomic nervous system. Their bodies did not effectively activate the relaxation response. Cortisol, an adrenal hormone released with the stress response, remained in the blood stream with deleterious effects. Cortisol "burns the furniture to save the house."[12] Many serious illnesses are precipitated by lingering stress hormones. The deterioration of the systems of the body is rapid within a body that is firing for survival and never finds safety. If threat is perceived as always present, the body responds accordingly. Within this context we can see how dis-ease in the mind can contribute to disease in the body.

---

[11] "Stress hardiness" was a term developed for research in the field of Psychoneuroimmunology (PNI). The field has since expanded to Phychoneuroimmunoendocrinology (PNIE).

[12] *Integrative Yoga Therapy Manual*, Joseph Le Page.

Autonomic Nervous System (ANS)

The ANS is the part of the central nervous system (CNS) responsible for maintaining homeostasis. The CNS consists of the brain and spinal cord. The ANS is a motor system independent of the motor system that controls somatic movement. It consists of two major divisions, the sympathetic and parasympathetic, which work together to regulate our internal milieu. Some examples are control of heart rate, digestive movement, respiration, thirst and hunger.

Central Motor Systems:

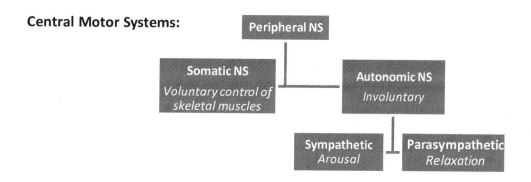

During heightened arousal, the body is oriented to attend to the external environment. Arousal under stress and the sustained energy for attending to the environment come from nerve impulses arising in the ANS. The sympathetic division of the ANS is reinforced by stimulation of the adrenal gland of the endocrine system, which acts as a kind of sympathetic ganglion.[13] Adrenal secretions of epinephrine, norepinepherine, and cortisol stimulate the heart, which causes peripheral vasoconstriction. Vasoconstriction increases blood pressure and helps mobilize blood to large muscles needed for running or fighting. Adrenal secretions also inhibit immune function. With sympathetic activation, digestion slows and the immune system is suppressed.

The ANS is by no means "automatic," in that it is under the control of higher brain structures such as the hypothalamus and the limbic system.[14] Arousal (and simultaneous inhibition of the parasympathetic division) is from the hypothalamus and pituitary with modulation from the pre-frontal cortex. The emotion of fear, for example, triggers a small body in the center of the brain called the amygdala, which, with modulation from the cortex, triggers hypothalamic activation of sympathetic arousal

Summary of Stress Response, the Sympathetic Arousal of the ANS
1. Perceived threat or challenge comes through various sensory messages (visual, auditory, etc.) which activate multiple brain structures, resulting in sympathetic arousal.

---

[13] A ganglion is a cluster of nerve cell bodies.
[14] The limbic system includes cortical/subcortical areas, which themselves regulate the hypothalamus and autonomic activity. It may be thought of as a high level emotional regulator.

2. This results in peripheral vasoconstriction. Digestion slows, the immune system is compromised, and the reproductive system is suppressed. The adrenal glands are stimulated to send hormones into the blood stream: epinepherine, and the sustained energy of cortisol. These hormones are steroids and give "hardiness" or sustained energy to the body after the nervous system has fired arousal.

3. Once the challenge or threat is over, the system needs to rejuvenate. The function of the parasympathetic division of the autonomic nervous system is to allow the body to recuperate and regain a normal homeostatic balance. Normal digestion resumes and the immune system can function effectively.[15]

   – The parasympathetic division of the ANS is responsible for renewal. This has been coined "the relaxation response."[16]

Relaxation Response, Parasympathetic Activation of the ANS

- The parasympathetic response may be taught through various relaxation techniques such as Bio-feedback, Transcendental Meditation, and yoga.[17]

- Even under "stressful conditions" one can learn to activate the relaxation response. Another perhaps more accurate view is that one learns to inhibit sympathetic arousal, or to turn it off sooner after it is no longer needed, which in turn results in greater activation of the parasympathetic division.

- The parasympathetic response is bi-neuronal, as is the sympathetic, but it fires to about 22 individual points in various organs of the body, a vastly smaller number than the sympathetic.

- A sustained experience of parasympathetic dominance and/or balance with sympathetic arousal is cultivated in the practice of yoga, particularly during deep relaxation.

The Amygdala

The amygdala is an almond-shaped ganglion in the center of the brain that is a part of the limbic system but lies just below it, within the temporal lobe. It is an essential player in our ability to respond to stress and distress. We have two distinct emotions, fear and anxiety, that are decoded by the amygdala. From the thalamus, we respond globally to environmental stimuli and ready ourselves for a response to potential danger. A loud noise can alert us via the thalamus and the amygdala to defend or flee. This is a short, imprecise but quick neuronal pathway. A longer, more precise route comes via the medial prefrontal cortex where the brain reacts to a specific stimulus and chooses a response based on stored past experience. To state these two conditions more simply, the first is a physical response to fear and the second is a mental response to perceived danger. The fear response emanates from the central nucleus of the amygdala, the

---

[15] Early studies in PNI by Kiecolt-Glazer showed that medical students at the time of exams had a suppression of killer T cells.

[16] *The Relaxation Response*, Herbert Benson.

[17] *Full Catastrophe Living*, Jon Kabat-Zin.

region that controls our bodily responses. Anxiety is triggered outside the center of the amygdala in a region responsible for emotion and behavioral responses that persist after the perceived danger has passed. The amygdala can de-sensitize itself to the conditioned response and make it extinct. The protein molecule, NMDA, is responsible for the extinction of the fear response. The body is prepared to de-condition itself and learn new behaviors. Once the pre-frontal cortex determines a course of action, it quiets the amygdala. The health of the amygdala is related with dopamine levels. With dopamine depletion due to cocaine abuse, internal mechanisms for mediating anxiety are stripped for the long-term.

Post-Traumatic Stress Disorder (PTSD)

In this condition the pre-frontal lobe (medial pre-frontal cortex) loses its ability to inhibit the firing of the amygdala (stimulated by the emotion of fear), which in turn activates sympathetic arousal via the hypothalamus. The pre-frontal lobe is an area of higher order function, i.e. it can distinguish real from imagined threat. The flooding of the brain with gluco-corticoids can damage the hippocampus (involved in learning and memory). Smaller hippocampal volume has been found in military veterans and adult survivors of childhood abuse.[18]

Research on the Deleterious Effects of Stress

The lingering effects of stress in the body are due to adrenal hormone secretion of cortisol combined with the muscular contractions that come from attending to perceived stressors. This is generally experienced as an elevated heart rate and muscular tension in the jaw, neck, shoulders, and lower back. The patterns of tension in the body vary between individuals and can reflect mental attitudes, occupation, and any repetitive patterns of motion.

In addition, since cortisol weakens the body, it may result in the appearance of congenital (from birth) weaknesses. Heredity meets environment. Dietary imbalances and/or excesses in behavior can tip the body in favor of disease. In other words, if one has a genetic pre-disposition for heart disease, under stressful conditions, heart disease may be precipitated. Lifestyle changes in diet and exercise have the reverse effect. They can slow and/or reverse the course of disease.[19]

The Impact of Chronic Stress on the Systems of the Body[20]

Muscles/movement
- Chronic contraction leads to postural strain and exaggerated misalignment.

---

[18] *Brain Work*, Dana Foundation, Nov/Dec 2004.
[19] *The Program for Reversing Heart Disease* by Dr. Dean Ornish promotes lifestyle changes, involving vegetarian diet and yoga.
[20] Compiled from *Integrative Yoga Therapy Manual*, Joseph Le Page, 1994.

- Spasms lead to decreased oxygen, which causes an anaerobic reaction and buildup of lactic acid. Lactic acid signals "stress" to the brain, which initiates more contraction.
- By contrast, relaxation of muscles enhances the parasympathetic response.
- Contraction in voluntary muscles restricts smooth muscle function.

Bones/structure

- Cortisol is detrimental to bone growth and health. It breaks down compounds in the bone to be used as energy in the "fight or flight" response. If cortisol remains in the blood stream, rebuilding of the bones is less likely to occur.

Ligaments and tendons/flexibility

- Cortisone weakens connective tissue.

Heart/circulation

- Like any other muscle, smooth arterial muscle can become chronically contracted due to stress, which results in a reduction of arterial flexibility. This increases the workload on the arteries and the heart. Chronic contraction of striated limb muscles can inhibit the return of blood through the veins.
- Cortisol increases cholesterol in the blood. Cholesterol assists with the production of energy during the stress response. Left in the blood stream it contributes to heart disease by clogging arteries and reducing blood flow, subsequently increasing the workload on the heart.
- Addictive substances, such as alcohol and tobacco, which some attempt to use in an effort to reduce the impact of external stressors, actually increase the risk of the hypertension and heart disease.

Lungs/respiration

- Chronic muscular tension attributed to the stress response leads to impaired respiration. Muscular tension due to sustained sympathetic arousal increases thoracic breathing and decreases abdominal-diaphragmatic breathing, which reduces overall health and well-being.

Immune/defense

- Under the effect of perceived stressors, the body produces elevated adrenal hormones, adrenaline and cortisol. Specific immune defenses are deactivated by the adrenal hormones.

Endocrine/hormones

- Stimulation of the release of adrenocorticol hormones under stress is necessary for survival. The balance of endocrine function is highly interrelated with the nervous system and perceptions of the environment. The regulation of the internal environment is a fine balance between too much and too little secretion, and dependent on feedback loops to regulate secretions. Chronic stressors can condition the body to imbalances that have long-term negative effects on health.

Digestion/assimilation

- Under stress, striated muscular contraction and reduced peristalsis[21] impede digestion. Peristalsis is partially controlled by a special subdivision of the ANS called the enteric division, specifically related to visceral activity. Under stress from the environment, digestion is inhibited. This results from ANS activity pushing outside homeostatic limits.

- In addition, the body has an intimate relationship between neuropeptide receptors in the lining of the bowels and neuropeptides in the brain. Mental distress is correlated with a condition in the bowels where inflammation, excess secretions, and a resultant acidic, corrosive environment have created distress in the alimentary system.

Stress and Yoga

Stress results in an abnormally high activation of the sympathetic division of the ANS. Most of the muscles activated by this system are smooth or involuntary. In addition, the ANS regulates the heart muscle and the combined smooth and striated muscle of the diaphragm. Does this mean we are helpless to control our internal environment? Yogis have been known to voluntarily control heart and respiratory rate. The first area of the body over which a developing yogi gains control is the heart and lungs.[22]

Summary of Benefits: Yoga and Homeostasis

Yogic breathing increases CO_2 and O_2. CO_2 keeps capillaries dilated so there is an increased blood flow to the tissues. O_2, a smaller molecule, alone would shrink capillaries and decrease blood flow, experienced in a condition called hyperventilation.

When the muscles relax, then the cycle of pain/contraction/further pain[23] is alleviated. For muscular-skeletal health, the body benefits from relaxation so that it can maintain healthy alignment. Yoga exercises the entire skeleton and encourages healthy bone strength, both compressive and tensile.

Connective tissue, the fascia, does not contract when the muscle contracts. It follows the muscle. However, it shrinks if not stretched. In yoga, alignment in the poses, particularly after an injury, assists the healing of the fascia in the direction of movement so that the range of motion from scar tissue is not lost. Fascia that lies in the direction of movement provides more strength and prevents further tearing. Healing connective tissue requires an ample blood supply. Adherent scarring against the lines of stress will have to tear apart again to re-heal in the optimum direction. Adjacent tissues that are

---

[21] Peristalsis is a series of involuntary wavelike contractions that moves matter through the alimentary canal.

[22] Chinese Medicine refers to the combination of circulatory and respiratory systems as the heart/lung meridian.

[23] When the body is in pain, it contracts. The contraction leads to a decrease in blood flow that reduces the flow of nutrients to the muscle, and excess waste. That, in turn, leads to muscle cell injury and inflammation, which leads to further pain and muscle contraction.

injured heal in a binding of separate but related muscles called adhesions. This condition of protein binding inhibits the range of motion and is alleviated with yoga.

To open up the circulation of blood to the tissues, the body benefits from the "squeeze and soak" effect of yoga postures.[24] After squeezing, the flooding of oxygenated blood cleanses the tissues and increases blood flow, which brings relaxation to chronic muscle contraction. The release simulates the relaxation response of the parasympathetic nervous system and assists the overall relaxation of mind and body.

The body benefits from massage not only to the voluntary muscles but also to all the smooth involuntary muscles of the internal organs and the muscles of the alimentary canal. Internal massage opens blood flow and assists the body in maintaining the optimum health of the organs. Stretching massages the arteries, veins, and heart muscle and supports optimum functioning of circulation. Stretching enhances lung capacity and increases blood perfusion and oxygenation. Stretching opens the bronchial tree, and helps those with asthma or lung damage.

The "squeeze and soak" aids the digestive system via spinal twists, forward bends, and a few arm balances. The abdominal *bandha* and abdominal pump actively massage the whole area of digestion. Side bending massages the liver, spleen, and stomach. Postures that open the solar plexus can help the pancreas. Spinal rocking and poses that isolate the area of the lower ribs massage the kidneys.

Decreasing stress levels enhances endocrine balance. With overuse of adrenals and pancreas, the fine tuning of hormonal balance is jeopardized. The stress hormones are not all bad. Without them we would experience no stress-hardiness, and have a reduced ability to jump out of the way of an on-coming car. The body needs a low level of steroids to deal with environmental stressors. Healthy sympathetic arousal is part of homeostatic balance. Relief from rheumatoid arthritis from yoga comes from the fact that regular exercise increases the body's endogenous production of cortisone from the adrenal cortex. This natural steroid can bring relief from pain. Cortisone output at low levels leads to symptom reduction.

Emotions and immune function have been correlated in the flow of neuro-peptides. In the work of Candice Pert, we can summarize the benefit of yoga as a release of the endorphins that override the body's negative responses and bring a sense of euphoria. The body has a natural positive state that calms emotions and gives a general feeling of safety and belonging. The endocrine system is stimulated by backbends in general, and the thyroid is impacted by shoulder stand, bridge, and fish.

---

[24] By restricting blood flow to an area while in a pose, the body readies itself to provide an increased blood supply when the pose is released.

The nervous system is improved by increased circulation. More accessible glucose reduces the sense of lethargy and sleepiness. Stretching re-educates the spinal column and brain to function optimally and to not settle for a level of functioning dictated by stress levels and patterns of holding tension. The release of endorphins due to yoga enhances the overall well-being and ease in functioning of the nervous system that enhances relaxation and amplifies the benefit of circulation.

The benefits of lifestyle change encourage lifestyle change. There is a positive feedback loop at work when lifestyle changes bring relief to a range of symptoms from mood disorder and sleeplessness to physical pain.

The Vagus Nerve

The vagus nerve is the 10th cranial nerve, exiting from the brainstem. The term "vagus" comes from Latin for "wandering" or "vagabond" because it travels far and innervates most organs. Stimulating the vagus nerve increases parasympathetic dominance (the relaxation response) and therefore is often viewed as the central command center for the parasympathetic nervous system. This important nerve is intimately involved with digestion, heart rate and breathing.

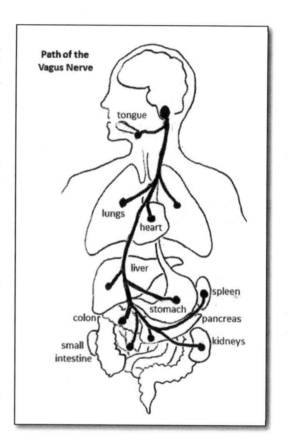

What we want is a good "vagal tone," meaning not too little or too much stimulation. Too much vagal activity has been associated with depression and a dangerously slowed heart[25]; too little vagal activity has been linked to poor stress resiliency and anxiety. A good vagal tone means we can recover faster from the "fight or flight" response, but are still able to act.

Vagal nerve stimulation[26] has long been a treatment in epilepsy and is currently being researched for a wide range of other conditions, including tinnitus, depression, PTSD and Alzheimer's. The National Institutes of Health has recently commissioned a study to examine the link between yoga and the vagus nerve, based on the hypothesis that yoga works because it increases vagal tone. Research conducted in 2013 that demonstrated the efficacy of ujjayi pranayama, chanting, and rocking suggested a link between vagus nerve stimulation and the positive outcomes of these practices.[27]

---

[25] In emergency clinical situations, a slowed heart is treated with a drug to inhibit the vagus nerve.

[26] Automatic VNS (vagal nerve stimulation) is done via a pacemaker-like implant.

[27] For more, refer to the National Institutes of Health website, NIH.gov, as well as these specific sources – *International Journal of Yoga*, 2013 Jan-June 6 (1): 4-10; *Journal of Current Biology*, 2013 April.

Some general ways we can work with the vagus nerve in a yoga practice:
- → *Twists and forward folds, massaging the innervated organs*
- → *Full, long breaths from the bottom up*
- → *Turning the head to look over a shoulder, stimulating the path through the neck*
- → *Unilateral, cross-crawl work*
- → *Vinyasa, generally moving body with breath, going into and out of postures*
- → *Ujjayi pranayama, either by itself or incorporated into postures*

Spend some time reviewing Gary Kraftsow's book, <u>Yoga for Wellness</u>, for more practice ideas.

Self-Maintenance and Self-Transcendence
An Emerging Model for Therapeutic Yoga

Yoga teaches us that if a system can transcend itself in meditation and reach to the highest organizing principle of consciousness, along with a dynamic, balanced circulation of energy, and relative quiet and harmony in the cerebral cortex, then self-maintenance will be optimal. This is consistent with current Physics[28] regarding the behavior of subtle matter.

- The theory of entities is that they are self-organizing and self-asserting.
- Every particle consists of all other particles.
- The whole is enfolded in each of the parts.
- To continue to understand matter we must include the effect of consciousness.
- Consciousness is part of the self-organizing dynamic.
- The rational mind recognizes order in the environment and organizes it according itself.
- "The consistency of the internal environment is the essential constituent of independent life" – the forerunning thought of homeostasis.
- Energy expresses itself in fluctuating systems.

Therapeutic Implications Allied with Systems Theory
According to systems theory, organizations that allow for the interrelationships of interdependent systems to fluctuate together are self-organizing and self–renewing. Holistic health treats the whole system. We treat people, not the "labels" of disease. People are experts in their own healing. As yoga teachers, we help them facilitate their own healing.

What yoga adds to the wealth of healing practices is a therapeutic lifestyle.

---

[28] *The Turning Point*, Fritjof Capra.

In the Face of Environmental Change

Sudden change: The system of the body is adaptable but rigid because of reaching a limit in fluctuation. With a sudden change in altitude, one cannot run up stairs without panting and fatigue.

Somatic change: Adapting to change will allow the system to move away from the limit and be less rigid, e.g. acclimatization.

Genotype change: This is the most adaptive response to long-term change, since there is a shift in the range of variables over time. Under adaptive change, more variables are left open to wider fluctuations, leading to creativity, power and evolution.

ASSIMILATION

Content

> Define these terms:

- Homeostasis

- Autonomic nervous system

- Sympathetic

- Parasympathetic

- Enteric

Contemplation

> When do you enjoy "stress?"

> What are a few problems you have when you get "stressed out?"

> What makes them problems?

> What are some shared stressors in the environment we live in?

> What is your relationship to time?

> What is your relationship to money?

> Is a "deficit mentality" a way in which the environment is perceived as a threat?

> Name other possible perceived "threats."

> What happens to your "stress" response when you sigh?

➤ Review the problem of stress and its impact on our autonomic nervous system in terms of the three gunas.

- What is a rajasic state?

- What is a tamasic state?

- What is their relationship?

- What is a sattvic state?

Personal Practice

➤ Experiment with breathing with a ratio of 2:1. Exhale 2: Inhale 1. (Count 6:3)

➤ Experiment with breathing with a ratio of 4:4. Exhale 4: Inhale 4.

➤ What are a few poses that teach mula bandha?

Poses

➤ Draw a series that is a preparation for pranayama

➤ Draw out a brief practice focused on vagus nerve stimulation. Consider a variety of pose categories – supine, prone, seated, standing:

*Renouncing entirely all desires born of volition,
and restraining the mind from all the senses on all sides,
little by little one should withdraw oneself from the objects other than the self
with the help of the intellect held by firm resolution;
then think of nothing else.
Bhagavad Gita 6/24, 25*

Chapter Eight – Restraint

*SS 11 The Five Souls of Action
YS II/28-45 Yamas and Niyamas
Begin assignment on Yamas and Niyamas
Written assignment due on the Nervous System, Brain, Yoga and Meditation*

The story of the eighth chapter: the souls of action —restraints, practice, detachment, a stable mind, and increasing insight—help us overcome our individual suffering. Lifestyle is key. With a balanced mind and a guiding intellect, we can maintain homeostasis in the face of challenges: a closer look at immune, endocrine, and digestive systems and how poses assist physiology.

Contents

PHILOSOPHY

Samkhya Sutra 11: The Five Souls of Action

Self-restraint, practice, dispassion, stable intellect, and wisdom give action focus and value for spiritual development. The first, self-restraint is *yama*, of which there are five: non-violence, truthfulness, non-deception, control of emotion, and non-accumulation. These five vows of self-restraint reduce our projection of energy into the environment and keep us in balance with others. With this containment the other souls of action can be fruitful. Practice and dispassion work together: we detach from outward craving and seek inwardly for the real self. The fruit is a stable, non-fluctuating intellect that can guide us with wisdom. These five give us clarity, right knowledge, and the energy for freedom. Otherwise, if we get caught in wrong knowledge and fancy, infatuation will keep us tied in the five knots of ignorance given in the next *sutra*.

The five souls of action begin with the *Yamas* (Y.S. II/30)	
Ahimsa	Non-violence or non-harming
Satya	Truthfulness or accountability
Asteya	Non-stealing or non-misappropriation
Brahmacharya	Self-restraint
Aparigraha	Non-accumulation or non-grasping

Non-harming comes with the growing realization that the same self is in all beings. Truthfulness and non-stealing come with acceptance of our place within energy. We do not need anything or any credit beyond the limits of our place. *Brahmacharya* is practiced as we watch the energy of our system and how it is used. Our most powerful stance is non-grasping and non-accumulation. If we can hold the fundamental vision of wholeness and oneness within both consciousness and energy, we are never separate beings and we are in no need of grasping and holding to complete ourselves.

Brahmacharya

Of these the least understood is *brahmacharya.* The traditional translation is celibacy or control of sexual energy. The literal meaning is "residing in the source." The meaning Swami Bawra gives is control of emotion. Emotion is energy. Energy is what courses through the body, sexual or emotional.

There is a verse in the *Bhagavad Gita,* "He who can tolerate passion and anger while in the body is wise among men; he is a yogi."[1] The power of fear and anger is not meant to be suppressed. But we fear its expression. It can be destructive. The answer lies in *brahmacharya,* control. We control water by creating channels for its flow. We control

---

[1] *Bhagavad Gita 5/23*

fire, by containing the flame with the fuel. Control of emotion is like controlling a natural force. Suppression is impossible. But not controlling the flow is destructive.

The first tool is observation. Tolerating anger and passion in the body means to watch it and observe it. Containment leads to a refinement of vision; it sharpens decisions and hones our actions. It is not to be spilled, but used respectfully as a power.

Emotions and the *Doshas*

If we look at the three basic emotions of fear, anger and grief, they are seated in the body according to the *doshas*. Fear is felt in the region of *apana.* The unseating jolt of fear sends energy up to the realm of *vata* in the chest. The persons best adaptive to fear are *kapha* types who tend to be heavy. Their stocky constitutions make fear less unseating of their equilibrium.

Similarly anger is felt in the region of *samana*, the center of the body. Anger sears through the body and threatens to blind the person feeling it. *Pitta* types contain anger best because the seat of their constitution is in the center of the body. *Pitta* types express anger as movement.

Grief is centered in the lungs and chest, the home of *vata* whose seat is low in the *kapha* region. Grief that is expressed in the body releases intense *prana*, and helps the *prana* move toward *apana.* Grief, letting go, frees energy for living in the moment.

Intense emotion comes through the body. Like all sensations, they are expressive of energy that takes a shape and gives us information. The emotion of fear protects us by mobilizing flight or fight. Anger is an indication of violated boundaries. Grief is an emotion that returns the system to homeostasis. All energy is part of nature; it is useful. What we practitioners wish to avoid is the unconscious harming of others that occurs when the emotion is not witnessed and understood. Emotion gives insight that in turn guides our behavior.

Kapil's five souls of action describe practice. The *niyamas* of Patanjali, the second limb of the eight-limbed path,[2] are missing from Kapil's *sutras.* The *niyamas* can be included as an expansion of practice and detachment. The *yamas* teach a healthy detachment from our external world and the *niyamas* support our inward search for the real self.

---

[2] *Yoga Sutras* II/31.

Niyamas, personal observances, the heart of a yogic lifestyle (Y.S. II/32)	
Saucha	Purity
Santosha	Contentment with perseverance
Tapas	Austerity – literally "heat," tolerating the intolerable (includes diet, breathing exercises, etc.)
Svadhyaya	Self-study, reading, meditation
Ishwara Pranidhana	Self-surrender

The practice of purity includes an orderly environment, a clean body, nourishing food and appropriate speech. Purity with simplicity supports our work and rest. Contentment comes with acceptance of what we have and the work we have done. We are satisfied, free of cravings. Then the intolerable frictions of life along with the restraints of our practice act as abrasions that free us of our outer identities. The search for the real self is guided by the inspiration of those who have gone before and with the use of inner sound, *mantra*. The fruit of the inner practice is surrendering inward and finding a quiet, focused awareness.

Lifestyle Change and Medicine

This traditional teaching of *niyama* encourages a lifestyle of detachment that has a physiological correlate. We are more balanced, settled in our lives, and accepting of restraint. This helps our bodies stay in homeostasis. Within medicine, activities that support our health and wellbeing are understood as preventive medicine. We are proactive – working to create balance rather than waiting to correct any imbalance of disease and distress. With yoga we are our own agent, not reliant on other experts to balance us.

The Eight-Limbed Path of Patanjali (Y.S. II/28-55)

Yamas	*vows:*
ahimsa	non-violence
satya	truthfulness
asteya	non-stealing
brahmacharya	control of energy
aparigraha	non-accumulation
Niyamas	*observances:*
sauca	purity
santosa	contentment, perseverance
tapas	austerity
svadhyaya	self-study
ishvara-pranidhana	surrender to source
Asana	postures
Pranayam	breathing exercises
Pratyahara	inward turning of the senses
Dharana	concentration
Dhyana	meditation
Samadhi	absorption (lit., evenness of intellect)

The eight-limbed path is a complete path that captures all diverse aspects of our human experience, from gross to subtle to causal. Diversity is the result of the manifold expression of energy.[3] Energy manifests from subtle to gross in eight layers that become the root of all expressions, all names and forms. We are an expression of the intermingling of energy and consciousness. Valuing both and separating out the intermingling is called yoga. The virtue of this knowledge is that we can see where we are on the path, and work specifically to untie the knots that keep us from finding our inner freedom. Change is the intrinsic quality of nature. Consciousness is inherently stable. As we find the stable ground of our awareness and identify less with the fluctuations of energy, we become free.

---

[3] Eightfold Nature is discussed in the Kapil's Sāmkhya, *sutra* 2. "There is Eightfold Nature."

METHOD

Truth, Non-harming, Yamas and Niyamas While Teaching

As teachers

We are models of the yogic path. As such, we do not have to preach the philosophy of yoga so our students can live the teachings. We need simply to teach in such a way that the observances and virtues can be naturally imbibed. Then as our students grow, their curiosity will bring them to an understanding of yoga that does not conflict with what they have already learned.

As such, our approach to others is that in a spirit of honesty we share the truth of the teaching in a generous, non-harming manner, bringing the light of our consciousness to bear on our shared experience of being human. We need to respect the boundaries of others, the essence of restraint and the control of energy, and we are beholden to share what we have both of material objects and of knowledge.

We teach in a clean environment, with an uncluttered approach to the knowledge. The unnecessary comparisons that complicate our minds should be avoided. In a spirit of sharing what we are learning, we express contentment for what we have—health and loved ones. Our difficulties are also shared. No one is free of challenges and the need to self-reflect, and we all share in the bounty of the wisdom that comes when we live closer to our real self.

As we live the teaching of the yoga, our students will directly benefit.

TECHNIQUE

Review physiology in "Asanas and Their Benefits - Annamayakosha Chapters 3,4,5,6.

Sequencing for the Immune System

Yoga assists lymph flow by stimulating the nodes in the groin, under the arms, and in the neck, and by increasing overall circulation through movement where muscles act like auxiliary lymphatic pumps. The spleen and thymus are stimulated equally in full bridge pose. The overall ease gained through practice assists the return to autonomic balance away from arousal into a state of restful alertness.

Standing breathing:

inhale   exhale (10x)   suspend   inhale   exhale (10x)   lengthen

slow descent   forward fold

Seated hit rotation:

       lengthen spine, soften hip   resting on elbow, open opposite hip

rest back on two elbows – swing around and hug side leg to chest   seated twist

butterfly with breath   seated butterfly

Standing hip work:

wide stance forward fold   "hey, batta, batta"   lunges...

side stretches

On knees:

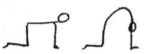  

table   cat   cow   sunbird   exhale

table inhale   extended child's exhale   c-curve

Bridge poses:

pelvic tilts   inhale   exhale   inclined bridge   full bridge
roll shoulders
under & breathe

Counterposes:

one knee to chest   rock spine   two knees to chest

  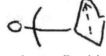 

pelvic clocks around   slow butterfly side to side (open & close a book)
the sacrum

plow   restorative bridge   deep relaxation

ANATOMY

Immune System

The immune system is an intricate system of cells and mechanisms that defend the body against infection (bacteria, fungus, viruses, and parasites), and is both specific and non-specific. We begin life with a non-specific response, known as the innate immune system or "first line of defense," that attacks in a generic way yet presents antigens to activate the more specific system. As we are exposed to pathogens, the adaptive or acquired immune system develops specific immunity and creates a memory that can provide lifelong protection against certain pathogens (this is the basis of vaccinations).

The immune system includes the lymphatic system[4] (an extensive network of vessels and nodes that transport lymph), the tonsils and thymus (which make antibodies), bone marrow (where white blood cells are made) and the spleen (which filters the blood). Antibodies and white blood cells identify, attack, and attempt to destroy bacteria and viruses that are deemed foreign invaders to the body's system. *Hatha yoga* assists the immune system by the movement of lymph that comes with complete breathing and the massaging of fluid through the tissues during the poses. Also, a direct result of a reduced stress response is the restoration of immune surveillance function.

How these parts work together to create the body's natural defense system:

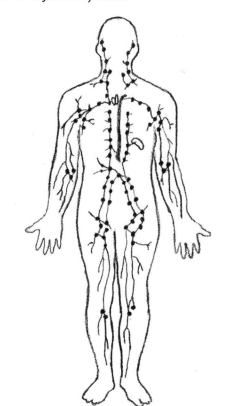

Lymph: The fluid that circulates through the lymphatic system, bathing the tissues of the body. It is made from interstitial[5] fluid and contains lymphocytes, hormones, nutrients and waste products that go from peripheral tissue into the blood. Two thirds of the lymph enters into a vein in the left shoulder area (note: tenderness and soreness in this area is correlated with immune function).

Lymphatic vessels: The extensive network of channels (pictured to the right as the lines running throughout the body) that carry lymph from the body's tissues to the venous system. Lymphatic vessels run parallel with blood vessels but are even more prolific. Unlike arteries, which have muscular walls, lymphatic vessels have walls of smooth muscle.

Lymph nodes: Organs of the lymphatic system (depicted in the picture to the right as the pronounced dots) that clean the lymph of pathogens. If the nodes

---

[4] Note that the lymphatic system is also considered a part of the circulatory system.
[5] Interstitial = the fluid between cells.

are not successful with their non-specific responses, the nodes enlarge as they lose the battle. The results are swollen tonsils, lacteals (intestinal), axillary (in the underarms), or inguinal (in the groin) nodes.

Lymphatic ducts: Vessels that drain lymph to the subclavian veins to return the material back into circulation. There are two in the body – the right lymphatic duct that drains lymph mainly from the right side, and the larger thoracic duct that collects the majority of the lymph that circulates through the body, transporting up to four liters of lymph daily. (The thoracic duct can be seen in the picture above as the central solid line by the sternum.)

Flow of lymph: Lymph has no viable pumping system other than the movement of the body. Muscles act like auxiliary lymphatic pumps, and varying body positions, particularly inversions, helps lymph to circulate. Breathing and massage also assist lymph flow. (Note: intense muscular contraction can be counter-productive).

Thymus: Organ of the immune system behind the sternum, near the motion of breathing. Lymphoid stem cells originating in the bone marrow travel to and mature in the thymus. T cells execute specific defense and memory T cells remain as sentinels. The thymus mostly deteriorates with age into a fibrous mass, contributing fewer and fewer cells with age (decreasing by 3% every year) and leaving us to rely more on what is already throughout the body. The effects of yoga poses on slowing the deterioration are unknown.

Spleen: Organ of the immune system said to be similar to a large lymph node. It is a mass of lymphoid tissue, near and under the stomach on the left side, that cleans the blood by removing old/damaged red blood cells. The spleen also synthesizes antibodies to fight infection and holds a reserve supply of blood for emergency needs. One can live without the spleen, but not without compromising the immune system. Yoga poses, especially inversions, massage the spleen.

Lymphocytes: Types of white blood cells that tour around in the lymph and blood stream looking for pathogens to engulf or otherwise demobilize. There are three classes of lymphocytes, all deriving from stem cells made in the bone marrow.
- NK cells – "natural killer," part of the innate immune system, non-specific lymphocytes that respond to general targets and are present in most tissues. They mature in bone marrow, lymph nodes, spleen, tonsils and the thymus gland. NK cells provide rapid response (within 3 days of infection) to virus cells and tumors.
- T cells – specific lymphocytes that are involved in cell-mediated immunity.[6] There are several kinds, including the most common "helper T cells" and "suppresser T cells." Some are toxic to cells and function like cancer treatment, killing cells. Cytotoxic T cells attack foreign cells, and cell bodies that have been invaded by

---

[6] Cell-mediated immunity means attacked by cells, without the aid of antibodies.

viruses. Helper T cells and suppressor T cells are involved with the regulation of the immune response. A helper T cell attaches to a B cell to synthesize antibodies.

- B cells – specific lymphocytes grown in bone marrow and part of antibody-mediated immunity. In combination with T cells, the presence of antigens (outsiders), and antigen presenting cells (e.g. a phagocyte), B cells are part of the specific response to antigens. Activated B cells produce plasma cells that produce antibodies, which are the exact antibody of the activated B cell.

Phagocytes:[7] These cells also originate in the bone marrow as white blood cells but are different from lymphocytes in that instead of fighting infection, they consume dead and dying cells and other debris in the blood. They also alert nearby lymphocytes of which antibodies are needed by release of chemical messages.

Antibodies: Protein molecules made by plasma cells (a type of white blood cells) that are specific to antigens and usually come with some variation, like a family, to capture the antigens.

Inflammation: One of the first responses of the immune system, designed to attract phagocytes, lymphocytes, and a host of chemical factors that trigger other mechanisms in order to provide a protective barrier against spread of infection, promote healing and cleanup of "carnage." Signs of inflammation include pain, swelling, redness, warmth.

The Immune Response has been compared to our national system of defense. The response requires surveillance, general response, and specific response. Once a danger has been met, systems remain in place to prevent further invasions. In other words, surprise is not likely the second time around. This is the basis of immunization.

Cancer is an error in cell replication. During normal development and in healthy adults, a process called apoptosis occurs by which damaged or unneeded cells self-destruct (programmed cell death). This is a natural and critical part of maintaining homeostasis. As with most systems and processes in the body, too little or too much is a problem. Too much apoptosis is implicated in Parkinson's and Alzheimer's, and too little with cancer. In the latter case, "rogue" cells that should have been destroyed instead proliferate.

---

[7] Phagocytosis means "ingestion."

Autoimmune Diseases

Autoimmune disease begins when T and B cells attack normal cells. These conditions tend to occur with greater frequency in women than in men. The chart below displays some of the more common autoimmune diseases and their primary affected areas:

Rheumatoid Arthritis	Joints
Crohn's Disease	Intestines
Multiple Sclerosis	Central nervous system
Type 1 Diabetes	Pancreas
Lupus	Connective tissue, organs, joints
Psoriasis	Skin
Grave's Disease	Thyroid
Hashimoto's Disease	Thyroid
Celiac Disease	Intestines

Rheumatoid Arthritis

Older yoga students will often have arthritis due to the wear and tear of activity in the joints. It is important to differentiate these conditions, gout and osteoarthritis, which are not auto-immune. Rheumatoid arthritis, on the other hand, is a major illness that is not life threatening. It affects the quality of life of over 50 million Americans. The main symptom is chronic pain due to swelling and restricted mobility in the joints. Gentle yoga is useful.

The average age of onset of rheumatoid arthritis is thirty-five. The symptoms are irritating to debilitating, expressed or in remission. The role of the immune system in the dysfunction is that antibodies cannot distinguish between healthy and infected cells and begin to attack healthy cells. The healthy cells respond with over-production. The joints become inflamed due to the swelling of tissue inside the joint capsule. The auto-immune response triggers a multiplication of synovial cells responsible for keeping the joint lubricated with synovial fluid. The cells implode the area of the joint and at further stages cause a decomposition of joint tissue of cartilage and even the bone itself. Deformity comes into the joints.

Benefits of Yoga

The weight bearing poses of yoga have been shown to stimulate the immune system. Inversions help move the lymph, as does the movement of the arms, deep breathing and stimulation of the calves.

Reduction in the firing of sympathetic arousal: The normal function of the immune system is maximal when the body is not chronically aroused. General benefits of yoga on the immune system come from the reduction in the excess of adrenaline (medulla) and cortisol (cortex) in the blood stream that is secreted by the adrenal glands during sympathetic arousal. Yoga practice balances the sympathetic and parasympathetic nervous systems, and the body is able to maintain normal homeostatic functions.

Adrenaline produces more energy by elevating blood sugar levels and increasing blood pressure. The problem with a chronic "high octane" level of functioning is when the body maintains this as a baseline it accelerates wear and tear. The complex immune system is given second place, as it were, during "fight or flight," and is intended to be resumed after the larger life-threatening, perceived stressors from the environment have ended. The problem is that perceived stressors might not go away from day to day.

Commuting to work can elevate blood levels of cortisol. Times of bereavement, moving to a new house, divorce, chronic pain itself are all stressors that can compromise immune function. Yoga helps us perceive the world differently and amplifies a condition called "stress hardiness."[8] There have been many studies on the effects of stressors such as loneliness (decreased NK activity), pessimism (decreased T cell and lymphocyte), and bereavement (lymphocyte) on specific immune measures.[9]

Asana practice also massages the various parts of immune function. Movement of lymph is amplified along with general blood circulation. The massage to the tissues and the movement of breathing act as a lymph pump, as an actual pump is missing from this systemic immune function. The massaging effect to the spleen, the thymus and the stimulation of the bones also boost immune function.

Endocrine System

The endocrine system is a collection of glands that produce and secrete hormones into the bloodstream to carry to distant cells or organs in order to regulate their activity. It is predominantly an information signaling system, producing slow to initiate but relatively long lasting effects. The hypothalamus is the neural control center for the endocrine system (refer back to Chapter 6 for CNS details). To regulate themselves, the secretions are directly or indirectly inhibited by negative feedback loops.

There are two primary types of communication within the endocrine system[10]– paracrine signaling and endocrine signaling. Paracrine signaling involves hormones traveling only short distances, producing "local" changes. These hormones alter a local tissue area by releasing lipoids into the interstitial fluids. These are called prostaglandins since they were first found in the prostate. They are released in response to inflammation due to allergies, cuts or bruises. Endocrine signaling travels further, via hormones that are secreted into the interstitial fluids and then diffusing into the bloodstream for transportation. Hormones are transported throughout the body and then diffuse back into interstitial fluids where they seek the receptors of target cells. Hormones are amino acids, proteins, or lipids.

---

[8] Early Research in Psychoneuroimmunology (PNI) on Medical Students during exams, Kiecolt-Glazer.
[9] *Integrative Yoga Therapy Manual,* 1994, Joseph Le Page, Mind-Body Health 7.45
[10] Secondary signaling - with autocrine signaling, the messenger binds to the other cell to produce changes, and juxtacrine signaling requires very close, physical contact to communicate and bring about changes.

Hormone communication is a slower and more sustained cellular communication than the nervous system. The sites of secretion are either organs/glands or tissues within the organ in the approximate areas of what in yoga are called the chakras. The sites listed below begin in the head and descend in order through the body.

Sites of Secretion

Pineal Gland: Produces melatonin in smaller quantities in the daylight and in greater quantities at night. The pineal gland is "light" sensitive – requiring light during the day and dark at night for proper function. Implied tasks include regulation of sleep and wake cycles, food intake and mood patterns, protection of the central nervous system from free radicals, and the slowing of maturation of egg, sperm, and reproductive organs.

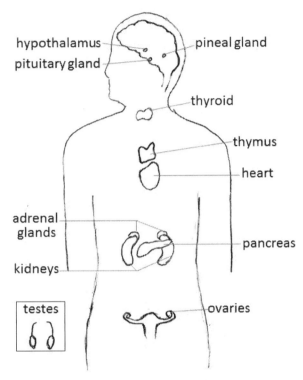

Hypothalamus: Secretes regulatory hormones that stimulate the release of additional hormones from the pituitary. Names correlate with and resemble the names of pituitary hormones. The hypothalamus also has direct neural communication with the adrenal gland as part of sympathetic arousal for "fight or flight."

Anterior Pituitary Gland: Produces the following hormones that stimulate other endocrine tissues throughout the body to release their hormones. The hormones are released from different cells in the pituitary.

GH - Growth hormone	Stimulates cell growth and replication by increasing rate of protein synthesis
TSH - Thyroid-stimulating Hormone	Low levels indicate a hyper-thyroid (too much) condition and vice versa
ACTH - Adrenocorticotropic hormone	Stimulates adrenal cortex and release of epinephrine (adrenalin)
PRL - Prolactin	Stimulates development of mammary glands (breast), also released during lactation. Sensitizes interstitial tissue to LH.
MSH - Melanocyte-stimulating hormone	Stimulates cells in skin to release melanin pigment. Increases during pregnancy & from birth control pills

FSH & LH - Follicle-stimulating hormone & Luteinizing hormone	Gonadotropins – development of eggs and sperm

Posterior Pituitary Gland: The posterior pituitary hormones affect non-endocrine tissues sites. The hypothalamus stimulates the posterior pituitary by neurons.

ADH - Antidiuretic hormone, aka vasopressin	Stimulates the retention of water is blood is too concentrated or if blood volume or pressure decrease. ADH prevents kidneys from releasing water in the urine, and causes contraction of peripheral blood vessels in order to elevate blood pressure
Oxt - Oxytocin	Promotes labor and delivery by stimulating smooth muscle of the uterus. Involved in reflex of infant suckling and milk ejection

Thyroid Gland: Produces thyroxine (T4) and Tridothyronin (T3), which contain iodine and regulate the rate of cellular metabolism. Skeletal muscles, liver and kidneys are affected as they are areas of high metabolism. Thyroid also releases calcitonin, which reduces calcium concentration in the tissues when elevated.

Parathyroid Gland: Produces parathyroid hormone (PTH), which increases calcium concentration when depressed. Since calcium is stored in the bone, PTH release stimulates removal of minerals from the bone and increased absorption from diet. (Located on the back of the thyroid gland.)

Thymus: Produces thymosins, part of immune function, that stimulate lymphoid stem cells to differentiate into various T cells.

Heart: Produces atrial natriuretic peptide (ANP), which lowers blood volume. This decreases the work on the right atrial wall that initially stimulated the release of the hormone. ANP reduces blood volume by simultaneously stimulating loss of sodium ions and water in kidneys, inhibiting water retaining hormones of ADH and aldosterone, and by suppressing thirst.

Adrenal Medulla: Produces glucocorticoids called epinephrine (adrenaline) and norepinephrine (noradrenaline), needed for the response to challenge, and to assist the breakdown of tissue proteins and lipids for fuel.

Adrenal Cortex: Produces mineral corticoids called cortisol, corticosterone, aldosterone, and androgens, related with making energy available to the body.

Pancreatic Islets: Produce hormones related with blood sugar levels.

Insulin	Released in response to eating and involved in the storage of energy. Elevated glucose in the blood stimulates the release of insulin. For anaerobic activity, muscle tissue and the liver store energy as glycogen. For aerobic activity, adipose (fat) tissue stores energy as triglycerides. Diabetes mellitus is a condition where insulin is not released or fails to stimulate energy. Hypoglycemia is a condition of excess insulin that depletes the blood stream of available glucose thus creating a condition of fatigue.
Glucagon	Involved in energy release along with epinephrine and cortisol. If glucose levels are low (after 4-5 hours of no food) glucagon is released. Glucagon stimulates the breakdown of glycogen and triglycerides and the making of glucose from amino acids (protein) at the liver.

Kidneys: Produce three hormones:

Renin	Involved in raising blood pressure in response to demands of stress.
Erythropoietin	Involved in energy release along with epinephrine and cortisol. If glucose levels are low (after 4-5 hours of no food) glucagon is released. Glucagon stimulates the breakdown of glycogen and triglycerides and the making of glucose from amino acids (protein) at the liver.
Calictriol	Released by PTH (parathyroid), stimulates absorption of calcium in digestive tract. Vitamin D is necessary for its production.

Digestive Tract: Produces gastrin, enterocrinin, secretin, cholecystokinin (CCK), somatostatin, and other peptide hormones.[11]

Gonads: Produce androgens (testosterone) in testes, and estrogen and progestins in ovaries. These hormones stimulate the development of eggs and sperm and secondary sexual characteristics, i.e. changes in vocal range, adipose tissue, hair growth patterns and muscle capacity. Inhibin is produced by both sexes to inhibit the release of FSH as part of a negative feedback loop.

The endocrine system is intimately interrelated with the nervous system, perception and association, conditioning, and immune function.[12] The main glands of the endocrine system are embedded in the brain. The release of these hormones into interstitial fluid assists the central nervous system and the autonomic nervous system to maintain homeostasis and face environmental change. Slight endocrine imbalances have an intense impact on health. It is possible to have a prolonged imbalance that eventually leads to a major illness e.g. hypoglycemia develops into diabetes (overproduction of insulin eventually leads to underproduction).

---

[11] For more on peptides, the body and the brain: The Molecules of Emotion, Candice Pert, Ph.D.
[12] As researched in the field of Psychoneuroimmunoendocrinology (PNIE).

As a response to stressors, the body prepares to act by making energy available for use. Thyroid and adrenal function increase the available energy of the body. Thyroxine and adrenaline have a similar subjective effect on our bodies of accelerated heart rate and rapid breathing with resultant exhaustion. Thyroxine amplifies the tissues response to adrenaline and lingers after the effect of adrenaline is gone. Thyroxine plays a part in our sustained response to prolonged stress.[13]

Stressors can have differing impacts on our nervous systems, one stressor inciting anger, another fear. The response of our nervous and endocrine systems together is acutely organized to meet the demands for energy and focus. The adrenal medulla has two hormones whose exact roles in varying responses are not understood.[14]

The HPA Axis

A major component of the stress response system is the HPA axis, or the "hypothalamic-pituitary-adrenal" axis, sometimes called the limbic-HPA because of the memory and emotional components involved. The HPA axis is a feedback system, which means it loops back to influence its own function.

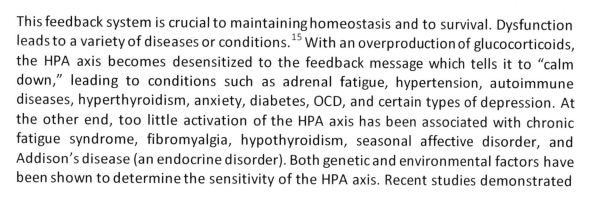

1. Homeostasis
2. Threat to homeostasis (physical or psychological stress)
3. Hypothalamus secretes corticotrophin factor (CRF)
4. CRF travels to the pituitary and triggers the release of adrenocorticotrophic hormone (ACTH)
5. ACTH travels through the bloodstream to the adrenals and triggers the release of glucocorticoids (cortisol, epinephrine and norepinephrine)
6. Glucocorticoids increase the availability of the body's fuel supply (carbs, fat, glucose) needed to respond to the stressor(s)
7. Glucocorticoids travel back to signal the pituitary and hypothalamus to turn off

This feedback system is crucial to maintaining homeostasis and to survival. Dysfunction leads to a variety of diseases or conditions.[15] With an overproduction of glucocorticoids, the HPA axis becomes desensitized to the feedback message which tells it to "calm down," leading to conditions such as adrenal fatigue, hypertension, autoimmune diseases, hyperthyroidism, anxiety, diabetes, OCD, and certain types of depression. At the other end, too little activation of the HPA axis has been associated with chronic fatigue syndrome, fibromyalgia, hypothyroidism, seasonal affective disorder, and Addison's disease (an endocrine disorder). Both genetic and environmental factors have been shown to determine the sensitivity of the HPA axis. Recent studies demonstrated

---

[13] *Mind as Healer, Mind as Slayer*, Kenneth R. Pelletier
[14] Ibid
[15] Greek endocrinologist, George Chrousos MD, is a leading researcher in HPA axis dysfunction diseases.

that children exposed to high levels of stress (prenatally or in early childhood) have an overly sensitive HPA axis that is set off more easily by smaller triggers.

Yoga and the Endocrine System

Yoga benefits the endocrine function in some known and other more obscure ways. A reduced dominance of the sympathetic arousal takes the endocrine system as a whole away from the brittle edge of exhaustion. Stimulation of the endocrine system through the pressure of the poses, especially backbends and shoulder stand, stimulate the integrated function of this finely interconnected system.

From the above information regarding the glands in the body and the powerful role of the hypothalamus and pituitary, we gain insight into the area between the brows, a focal point in meditation practice. Not enough is known about the impact of yoga and meditation practice on endocrine function but indications are that less medication is needed, such as thyroxin for hypothyroidism or insulin for diabetes.[16] The implication is that the practice of yoga assists the balance of the body toward a healthy homeostasis.

The special role of the light-sensitive pineal gland is indicated in yogic literature, but overall, the power of the body to find a more sustained source of energy as a result of practice is not understood.[17] In yogic literature, the role of endocrine function in supporting longevity and the subjective experience of a more sustained energy is indicated by the knowledge of the chakras,[18] but the physiology is as yet unknown.[19]

Digestive System

The Digestive System breaks down food into nutrients the body can assimilate. The nutrients provide energy and waste products are eliminated from the system. The digestive system is a long digestive tract in which a variety of digestive processes occur, both mechanical and via digestive secretions. The tract has the assistance of accessory organs such as the liver, pancreas, salivary glands, teeth and tongue. They break down food mechanically, secrete enzymes, and add water and substances that assist the process of absorption of nutrients through the mucous lining of the digestive tract.

During *asana* practice, forward folds and spinal twists massage the organs of digestion. The action of peristalsis is directly assisted by these movements, and digestive health is re-enforced by the increasing equanimity of the practitioner.

---

[16] *Yoga Basics: Yoga Therapy for Diabetes (Type II).*
The Psychological and Physiological Effects of Meditation: A review of Contemporary Research with a Comprehensive Bibliography (1,600 studies), 1931-1996.
[17] *Pseudoscience and the Brain:* Tuners and Tonics for the Aspiring Superhuman, Barry Byerstein.
[18] *Via Kundalini:* Psychosomatic Excursions in Transpersonal Psychology.
[19] *The OHNO Insititute*: Bio-magnetic Hydrology and Longevity; *Vibrational Medicine for the 21st Century*, Ronald Lynch, M.D., *The Web of Life*, John Davidson, 1988.

The Digestive Tract

1. Mouth, teeth and tongue prepare food by breaking it down and mixing with salivary secretions. Digestion of carbohydrates begins in the mouth with the secretion of the enzyme ptyalin.

2. The esophagus is a muscular membranous tube that lies between the pharynx and the stomach, and lies behind the trachea (lungs). It creates a lubricant that aids the passage of food. Swallowing closes the epiglottis so that food does not enter the trachea (the coughing reflex is the second line of defense).

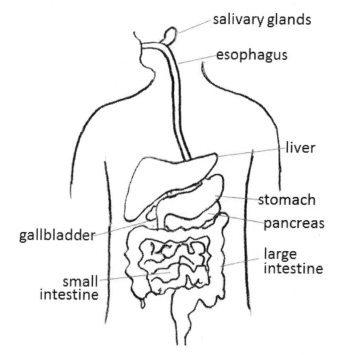

3. The stomach expands as food enters. It is a large muscular sac that lies above the small intestine. The stomach churns the food particles and liquidates them while secreting acidic compounds that further break down protein molecules. Pathogens are unlikely to survive this stage.

4. The small intestine is a slender, lengthy (3.5 X body length) tract composed of three segments. Just past the pylorus, the valve at the end of the stomach, comes the duodenum, then the jejunum, and before the entry to the large intestine, the ileum. Into the small intestine come secretions from the pancreas and the liver, via the gall bladder. The pancreas secretes protease for protein, amylase for carbohydrates and lipase for fats. The liver secretes bile that aids in the digestion of fatty compounds. Capillary beds surrounding the small intestine supply oxygen for the multiple conversions of food to energy, and receive molecules for transport of nutrients to the tissues. Good circulation to the belly is vital for good digestion. Note that under times of stress this supply is truncated to allow the peripheral muscles to act efficiently.

5. The large intestine absorbs, water, vitamins, and minerals as waste products of digestion are shunted toward the colon, where it waits for excretion through the rectum.

A system of valves is in place lying between the various organs/stages of digestion to prevent the back flow of digestive matter in the opposite direction. Digestion is linear. Any reversal is not only toxic but often painful because of digestive acid. In yoga the term "gastric fire" is used to describe the intensity of heat and energy released during digestion. Our digestion is like a furnace.

The digestive process includes smooth muscle activity within the gut. Wavelike contractions result in peristalsis, which helps move food along. These waves of muscular contractions are under autonomic control, but are also dependent on a group of nerves intrinsic to the gut muscle itself. These nerves are part of a virtually independent system called the "enteric nervous system."

Recent research has correlated the presence of peptides in digestion with neuro-peptides in the brain, thus establishing, in their view, a direct brain-body connection. Emotional distress directly effects digestion.[20] It is interesting to note the amount of common language that refers to digestion. "I can't stomach it." "I had butterflies in my stomach." And it has long been an adage, "You'll worry yourself sick."

Digestive Diseases

Although some have a genetic component, the stress response exacerbates these conditions.

Acid reflux	Burning sensation as gastric acid goes back up the esophagus due to some abnormal contractions of the stomach, or to problems with the esophageal sphincter, sometimes due to a hernia.
Gastric ulcer	Ulcer (an inflamed area with necrotic lesion) in the mucus membrane lining the stomach.
Gastritis	Chronic or acute inflammation of the stomach.
Duodenal ulcer	Ulcer in the small intestine.
Crohn's disease	Painful inflammation of small intestine and diarrhea, due to an auto-immune response in the intestines; can lead to severe osteoporosis.
Ulcerative & spastic colitis	Aka IBS (irritable bowel syndrome); ulcers and painful spasms in the smooth muscles of the colon and a resultant inability to derive maximum benefit from the action of the large intestine
Diverticulitis	Inflammation, infection and possible puncturing of the intestine walls due to trapped food particles; painful and fatal if ignored.
Colon cancer	Recently linked to meat proteins in the diet; previously linked to fat content in the diet.

Yoga poses that massage the organs of digestion are forward bends, twists, and arm balances like crow. Compression and release activates the "squeeze and soak" effect – first deprivation, then dilation of vessels in response to compression. The internal mental stability that arises from practice is an extremely valuable digestive aid.

---

[20] *The Molecules of Emotion*, Candice Pert, Ph. D.

ASSIMILATION

Content

➢ List and learn yamas and niyamas in Sanskrit and English

Contemplation

➢ From your reading, can you explain why we get colds when we have not had the time to "slow down?"

➢ Does your knowledge of the endocrine system explain more of how mental balance and physical health are correlated? How so?

➢ How does your "stomach" respond to stressors?

Personal Practice

➢ What are some of the unconscious ways we address our physiology during our practice?

➢ Can we make those more conscious?

➢ Can you make your breathing an integral part of working with the involuntary motor systems of the body?

Poses

➢ Find a few poses for the immune, digestive, endocrine systems. Draw them here.

During practice, the subdued mind of a Yogi
is as a lamp in a windless place that does not flicker.
Bhagavad Gita 6/19

Chapter Nine – Space and Wind

Written assignment due on Yamas and Niyamas
Written paper due on the Value of Yoga

The story of the ninth chapter: revisiting inversions and balance, and a look at the power of language to sculpt experience during asana.

Contents

Bless the mouth
For it is the describer
Bless the tongue
For it is the maker of words
Mary Oliver

215

Language is a sculpting tool. The clay is awareness.
The object of the art is to find ourselves.

METHOD

An Exploration of Boundaries and Space

Perceived Boundaries

Space is defined as the unlimited or incalculably great three-dimensional realm or expanse in which all material objects are located and all events occur.[1]

Space is just space; it is all-pervasive. We partition off areas and call certain spaces "my house," "my room," "my land," and yet space truly cannot be divided. In a similar manner, spirit or consciousness is all-pervasive and is only perceived to be limited by individual beings. The same spirit enlivens all individual *chittas* and, as one space pervades all rooms and other "divisions," spirit remains unchanged. It is like the sun that shines its rays in all directions and yet each ray remains connected with all other rays of light. We share such limitless connection with life and yet our limited forms are also our personal containers for experience and emancipation.

Necessary Boundaries

As teachers we must practice maintaining boundaries with students. Many become yoga teachers out of compassion—the wish to help others minimize suffering and find freedom. We wish to share the expansive experience of freedom from limitations. Students may sense our compassion and knowingly or unknowingly take advantage of us, perhaps by looking to "the teacher" to fix their problems, physical or psychological. As teachers we need to observe the boundaries of who we are.

For many, this will likely take much practice. Consider these points:

→ What is the purpose or value of the ego? What role does it play in your life? Are you merely the ego, the agent, or are you something more? Can your identity rest with your seer rather than your doer?

→ Always evaluate and reevaluate why you are a teacher. What is your intention? Ask yourself, "Why am I teaching this class, here, right now?"

→ Let the guiding principle be to equip your students to lead their lives well, to find their own sage guidance, rather than to depend upon you.

---

[1] Dictionary.com

→ Do your own work—dhyana (meditation), svadhyaya (self-study), and satsang (surrounding yourself with a practicing community, that is, others who are working on themselves).

→ Notice how boundaries play out in your own life—with close family, extended family, friends, co-workers, and neighbors. Observe how and where you need limits. Can you express those well and in a non-harming fashion?

→ Consider the value of containment, of pulling in, as well as the value of moving out to share with others.

→ Be comfortable with what you do not know and in saying, "I don't know." Know when to give referrals to medical professionals. Accept the fact that you cannot possibly have all of the answers all of the time. We have a few good answers some of the time.

→ Remember that you are sharing your knowledge, giving ideas, guiding students and keeping them safe, but that ultimately each person (student and teacher) is responsible for his or her own work toward inner freedom.

Language as "Wind in Space"

Language can help us feel spacious in the same way the wind blowing upon us helps us feel the space that surrounds us. The experience of sound and vibration can open us to the space we share. The forms we see are merely visible expressions of energy, vibrant and alive. Our speech is a form of energy, but one that is not trapped into any shape. Language is fluid, in that almost just as it is received and imbibed, it is instantaneously re-interpreted to fit the mind of the receiving ears. Language is not fixed. Yet, this is our primary medium of expression for our students. Language is like wind in space. And, as our students respond to our words, our language shapes their experience. As you speak, all that you are, all that you practice, all that you value will be conveyed through your expression.

Breath as Subtler than Language

As you breathe, you teach. If you practice creating a subtle experience of the breath and the mind, you will be able to take your students to a deeper place in themselves. Our starting point for this course was how to understand the breath, the spine and our energetic systems. At this point in your journey toward becoming a teacher, plumb the deeper intrinsic values of the shared values of space and breath that are activated by practice.

Teaching and the Spoken Word

Sensitivity to language grows with practice. The purpose of this section is to enlarge our comprehension of sound and develop more refined tools of speech.

There are two levels of speech: the accepted definition of words, and the received meaning, which is also felt. The gap between the accepted definition of language and the received meaning creates tension in speech. A close correlation of vibration with meaning leads to greater impact. This correlation is understood in Sanskrit, which is a language in which the terms and the vibration of the intended object correlate. The traditional understanding of the world of experience is contained in the terms *nama rupa,* or name and form. Name is the vibration of form, is subtler than form, and precedes the emergence of form into matter.

The formative imagination of the mind is called *sankalpa.* Our formative imagination is made more concrete during speech. Speech is a bridge from thought to action. What we project into the future through our speech begins to shape us in the present. We say of those who are conscious of the power of the bridge of speech, "Their word is good." They understand how to bring thought into form through speech.

According to Sāmkhya philosophy, life projects into form through a progression of elements, each successive one emerging from the others. Space contains in subtle form all the ones that succeed it. From subtle to gross the progression is:

Element	Sense	Chakra
Space	Sound	Throat
Air	Touch	Heart
Fire	Sight	Solar plexus
Water	Taste	Sexual center
Earth	Smell	Base of spine

The science of sound includes outward sound and inward sound. A *mantra* is an inwardly repeated sound whose intended purpose is to refine awareness by refining thought. Sound, moving through space, is related with the highest chakra and the subtlest sense, and by using sound in meditation the mind can reach a subtle state. Sound reaches back to the root of form in the vibration of energy. *Akasha,* or space, is the medium for the movement of sound. The experience of the element of space is the most akin to the experience of the higher Self, our essential being that is free of limitations.

Breath also takes us inward. Conscious breathing helps to release identification with the body. Then we can travel inward through the subtler layers of experience, *koshas.* As our awareness turns farther inward our awareness becomes increasingly subtle, refined, peaceful, and universal. When we link *mantra* with breath, outwardly through chanting and inwardly in mental repetition, our experience of refinement is enhanced. Breath is an elevator that can take us from the deep, dark sea of the body to the outer limits of space.

> *Look for the breath within the breath.*
> *Kabir*

Words can create the sensation of magnetism or shock

Spend some time moving a friend's body by shocking the limbs with a light touch. Have her hold the position she finds herself in and shock lightly again. Sculpt for a while this way. Then try magnetism, where she will follow your touch to create a new position.

Exploration of languages:

Language of earth	plant, drop, release, horizon, sink, settle, root, ground
Language of water	melt, depth, wave, flood, float, soak, flow, spring, rinse, wash
Language of fire	rise, amplify, shine, glow, light, illumine, kindle, brighten, radiate, simmer, warm
Language of touch & proprioception AIR	press, respond, drape, soften, sensation, wrap, gather, envelope
Language of space	elongate, expand, open, find, lengthen, reach, journey, scan, sense, vast
Language of observation	notice, observe, watch, see, feel, be, listen, tune-in, scan
Language of physiology	What are the benefits of details? How much? How little?

Language of discrimination	intend, focus, find, observe the difference between..., compare, select, discern, notice, limit
Language of compassion	hug, accept, open, embrace, invite, welcome, gently, freely
Language of ownership vs. detachment	'your hand' vs. 'the hand' how & when do we exercise choice around this?
Use of pronouns, singular or plural	'your' vs. 'our'
Language of stillness	value the pause, add the details of the pause
Language of kinetic movement	draw upon, work, wiggle, back & forth, active, lead & follow, initiate, sway, extend
Language of metaphor	e.g. fruit, plants & gardening: grow, core, peel, seed, sow, till; or flying: soar; or cleaning: rinse, wring-out
Value of humor	lightens the work, eases judgement, creates community
Language of paradox	feel the tension, stay with the discomfort, feel the dynamic opposition, *sthira-sukha*, (builds mental stamina) Stable easy
What to avoid	Language of perfectionism Language of shame and domination

TECHNIQUE

Asansas and Their Benefits: Pranamayakosha & Manomayakosha

Five *Vayus* – the winds
(Also refer back to Chapter 7.)

Udana
Circular movement through head and throat.
Communication and cognition.

Prana
Upward movement in heart, lungs and chest.
Peace and freedom from lethargy.

Samana
Central energy of digestion.
Digestive fire and organs.

Apana
Abdominal area and downward flow.
Elimination, menstruation, and childbirth.

Vyana
From core to every cell.
Peripheral Nervous System and circulation.
Food and breath to cells.

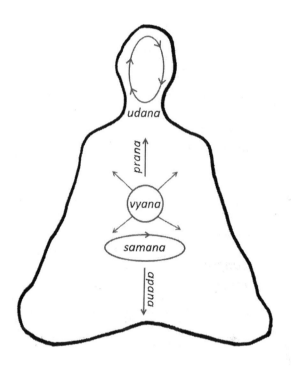

The five winds activate physiology and when the flow of prana feels vital, our physiology is supported. At the same time, our mental state shifts to greater clarity, concentration and positivity.

Forward Folds
Pranamayakosha
→ Activate *apana, prana, samana* and *udana, vayus.*
Manomayakosha
→ Enhance concentration and promote physical and mental relaxation.
→ Stimulate intellectual capacity by relieving lethargy and mental sluggishness.
→ Alleviate depression and insomnia.
→ Help develop mental poise and inner balance.

Twists

Pranamayakosha

→   Activate *samana* and *prana vayus.*

Manomayakosha

→   Release of mental tension.

Lateral Bends

Pranamayakosha

→   Open *samana*, *vyana vayu* and *prana* vayus.

Manomayakosha

→   Alleviate anxiety and hypochondria.

→   Reduce mental stress

Hip Range of Motion

Pranamayakosha

→   Open *apana* into *prana vayus.*

Manomayakosha

→   Quiet mind and emotions.

→   Give a feeling of safety, comfort, and steady centering.

Standing Poses

Pranamayakosha

→   Open all *vayus.*

Manomayakosha

→   Build stamina and confidence.

→   Create a wakeful, centered state of being.

→   Give grounded, steady and secure feelings.

Standing Balance Poses

Pranamayakosha

→   Emphasize *samana vayu*, also, *prana*, *vyana*, and *apana vayu.*

Manomayakosha

→   Develop single-minded focus for meditation.

→   Create mental awareness and poise.

→   Activate inner balance and peace.

→   Activate feedback loops in brain, cerebellum, vestibular function, and eyes supporting a feeling of integration.

Back Bends

Pranamayakosha

→ Stimulate *samana vayu*, with *prana*, *vyana*, and *udana vayus*.

Manomayakosha

→ Help regulate moods and emotions.
→ Relieve stress response and mental agitation.
→ Regular practice improves internal balance, harmony and clarity of mind.
→ Strengthen concentration and determination.
→ Awaken full potential

Inversions

Pranamayakosha

→ Activate *prana, udana, apana* and *samana vayus*.

Manomayakosha

→ Alleviate depression and insomnia.
→ Enhance physical and mental relaxation.
→ Develop mental poise and inner balance.
→ Improve communication and intuition via throat and fifth chakra.

Arm Balance Poses

Pranamayakosha

→ Activate *samana vayu*.

Manomayakosha

→ Develop power of concentration to prepare for meditation.

Sequencing for Beginners

Within the following sequence for beginners, observe how the various systems of the body are benefitting from the poses. Observe the effects on the pranamayakosha and the manomayakosha.

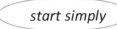 *start simply*   *eyes closed*   *reflect inward*

Breathe lying down or standing (see next page for standing breathing)

Breathe with the spine:

neutral   inhale   exhale (scoop)   inhale   exhale   neutral

1- knee to chest   2- spinal twist   3- supine crescent moon   4- knee to chest
& knee circles

On knees: table   extended child's   cat   long spine

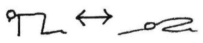   

inhale   exhale   exhale   inhale

1- tiger stretch

exhale   inhale & hold   exhale   rest

2- sunbird

exhale   inhale & hold   exhale   rest

3- C-curve

224

4- down dog   counterpose- extended child's

5- cobra   boat   sphinx   counterpose- extended child's

Breathing standing:
Breath of Joy – 3 sips in, 1 deep exhale

neutral   in... forward arms   in... wide arms   in...arms up   exhale arms back

1- flying bird forward fold (ff)

start w/ length   inhale lengthen spine   exhale ff & hang   inhale up

2- half moon (shoulders)

Exhale 1 arm forward   inhale arm back... rotate arm up   exhale crescent moon

3- wall hang (shoulders & hips)

start   step back   breathe...

4- runner's stretch (hips)   5- low warrior I

6- warrior II

7- modified triangle

8- side angle

9- wide stance forward fold

parallel feet

10- devilish hip opener (on knees)

calves & thighs square

11- pigeon (bent leg open, back
    leg tucked under)

12- counterpose (swing back leg from behind
    and cross it over front knee)

Rest:

1- on back with legs up the wall,
    hips elevated on a pillow

2- with a low bolster under back,
    shoulders & hips on the ground

3- deep relaxation pose,
    always finish with a few minutes
    lying on the back

Only that day dawns to which we are awake.
Thoreau

ASSIMILATION

Content

➢ Use your understanding of anatomy and physiology to assess what systems of the body benefit most from the following categories of poses? Look at the immune, endocrine and digestive systems.

- Forward folds

- Twists

- Lateral bends

- Standing poses

- Inversions

- Back bends

Contemplation

➢ How can we tell we are at risk for becoming out of balance? What are our personal cues?

Personal Practice

➢ Add your own physiological needs to your practice.

Poses

> ➤ Draw a series for one system of the body.

Poses

He whose mind is fixed in Yoga sees equality everywhere;
he sees his self as abiding in all beings and all beings in his self.
Bhagavad Gita 6/29

Chapter Ten – Meditation

Samkhya Sutra 12 – 15 The Five Knots of False Knowledge & the Twenty-Eight Inabilities
Yoga Sutras II//3 - 11 The Klesas
Yoga Sutras I/30 – 39 The Obstacles and Overcoming Them
Written assignment researching an aspect of the Immune System, particularly auto-immune conditions

The story of the tenth chapter: meditation is our starting point and our continuing point. It teaches concentration and sustained focus. If we have obstacles and ailments, it is our one-pointed focus and intention toward a viable solution that will serve us. Active listening skills help the teacher retain personal boundaries in the face of the suffering of others. Yoga is a method for assisting emotional health.

Contents

PHILOSOPHY

Samkhya Sutra 12: The Five Knots of False Knowledge

Darkness, infatuation, great infatuation, aversion, and blind aversion bind us to ignorance of the real self. Darkness of disconnection with the source covers the intellect. Then the ego becomes infatuated with itself, since it does not see its source in light and knowledge. Then attraction to outward objects and relationships take precedence over the real self. With attractions come aversion, and fear of loss, and finally the great fear of death.

Yoga Sutras II/3 – 11: The Klesas

The Five Knots of False Knowledge are also Patanjali's Klesas, the Miseries (Y.S. II/3-11)[1]

Avidya	Attaching the purity of seeing to the fluctuations of the seen and believing that the seen is all that there is.
Asmita	Asserting the ascendancy of the ego as the center of our being and believing that our intelligence is our own.
Raga	Attractions.
Dvesa	Repulsions.
Abhinevesa	Desire for life, and fear of loss of control and death.

According to Sāmkhya and Yoga, what makes the path integrative is finding the seer, and separating out the seer from the seen. When we identify ourselves with the seen (sanyoga) we feel a sense of separation from self, and we gather all the attendant feelings of being disconnected, dismembered, diseased, and distracted. When we come closer to the seer (yoga) we feel integrated. The separation of seer and seen (viyoga) is needed. The self we seek is consciousness itself. The goal is one. There are many paths because there are many seekers. The eight-limbed path is for all seekers. We remove the five knots of ignorance.

These miseries are ended and to be avoided by meditation. Patanjali outlines this in the following sutras which constitute his version of Samkhya philosophy with the Yoga Sutras.

> II/10   The root causes of pain in their subtle form are to be ended by inward propagation.

---

[1] The five *klesas* of Patanjali are elaborated in the second chapter of the *Yoga Sutras*, verses 3-11. The five knots of ignorance of Kapila are *tama, moha, mahamoha, tamisra, and andhatamisra.*

II/11   By meditation, the five causes of suffering can be annihilated.

II/16   The pain that is not yet come is to be avoided (heya).[2]

II/17   The cause of what is to be ended (heya) is the identification of the seer with the seen (sanyoga).

II/18   The seen, which has the three attributes of light (sattoguna), movement (rajoguna), and stability (tamoguna), projects in the form of elements and senses and is for experience and emancipation.

II/21   The whole seen in existence is for that seer.

II/24   The reason for that (identification of seer and seen in sanyoga), is ignorance (avidya).

II/25   With the disappearance that (avidya) comes the disappearance of sanyoga, that is, the end of suffering (hana) and liberation of the seer (kaivalya).

II/26   Pure and doubtless discriminative knowledge (viveka) is the way to the end (of suffering).

Samkhya Sutras 13 – 25: The Inabilities

Sutra 13: Twenty-eight-fold inabilities
These keep us in ignorance. Thirteen are handicaps within the ten cognitive and active senses, the mind, ego and intellect.

Sutra 14: Nine-fold satisfactions
Of the twenty-eight-fold inabilities, five keep us from applying effort: contentment with the pleasure of the five senses, and complacency that nature, and the ideas that the right time, means and luck will take us forward.

Sutra 15: Eight gifts or perfections
The final eight inabilities are a lack of any of the eight gifts that assist us: wisdom, sound or *mantra*, study, divine grace and service, and an experience of freedom from the three kinds of suffering. Without a real experience of the goal, we are uncertain. A real experience brings doubtless striving and firm faith, *shraddha*.

Yoga Sutras I/30 – 39: The Obstacles and Overcoming Them

Patanjali give a differing list of obstacles in verses I/30 and 31. Disease, dullness and doubt are related with various koshas. Laziness and a lack of detachment are related

---

[2] *Heyam dukam anagatam.*

with a lack of self-discipline. Pain and depression, trembling and difficulties with breathing are related with impurities in the body. He advises in I/32, a one-pointed practice and then in the remaining verses, suggests practices for specific issues.

METHOD

Self-study and Active Listening

For groups to have a healthy dynamic, teachers need to understand themselves.

Our training has two main emphases, alignment and homeostasis. The first section dealt with alignment on all levels: alignment in the poses, aligning with ourselves, and teaching healthy alignment to others. When we find healthy alignment, we resonate with it. Homeostasis is similar. We have to find it before we can teach it. Homeostasis is the term for how the body maintains a healthy internal environment, including metabolism, blood pressure, heart rate, hormone levels, and sleep/wake cycles. Homeostasis is maintained by the involuntary motor system called the autonomic system. In contrast with our voluntary sensory-motor system, which is primarily conscious, this involuntary system is primarily unconscious. Through the practices of yoga we appreciate the total sensory-motor system and become more aware of how unconscious feedback, bracing, synergy, timing and reflexes support our movement. Similarly through the practices of yoga, we enhance the health of the internal environment by consciously partnering with the involuntary motor system.

Homeostasis is maintained by the body, but the mind plays a critical role. For instance, the evaluation of our environment determines whether we fire the stress response. If we perceive a challenge as a threat, our nervous system will fire a state of arousal recruiting adreno-cortical hormones for sustained energy. These hormones, if not cleared from our system, create wear and tear in the inner environment. Homeostasis is compromised. If we perceive a challenge as interesting and exciting, we stay calmer and experience less wear and tear. Our internal physiological systems are constantly fluctuating in response to our thoughts and activities. Our bodies will seek homeostasis through all storms of activity. We can help our bodies find homeostasis through yoga practices.

With the yogic practice of self-study, we learn to observe our patterns of responding, which creates choice. With the ability to choose, we can support the activity of the involuntary systems that are seeking to keep us in balance. The choice is found in the pause and in the breath. Through the practice of conscious breathing we develop the capacity to access a calm reflective mental state, the basis of self-study. In deep relaxation and in meditation we have the opportunity to relinquish our habitual patterns and refresh our approach to life. In deep relaxation we rest. In meditation, because sitting initiates a state of wakefulness, we need a subtle focus to maintain a restfully alert state. Within deep relaxation and meditation we can observe our patterns of thought.

Outside of relaxation and meditation we expand our self-study to listening to our speech and witnessing our actions and reactions. Self-study is not easy because our sense of self is defined by habitual patterns of responding. We cannot always see our patterns; we have to accept hints from our environment concerning our speech and actions. No matter how good our intentions, our speech and behavior imperfectly display them. The following list of terms is an exercise in self-study. As teachers of yoga, the more self-knowledge we have, the more we can be of service to others.

Spend some time finding yourself in the following terms.
It is always easier to see patterns in others, but then look for how you manifest them.

Authenticity is being true to self. We feel our feelings. We believe our own thoughts. We speak as clearly and truthfully as we can, and we strive for our actions to reflect our beliefs.

A **boundary** is a place where we negotiate between self and world. A healthy boundary is porous, allowing information to pass in and go out. This is in contrast to a wall which is rigid.

Defenses work to protect us from our own feelings. Examples are withdrawal, intellectually defending, blame or deflection, and humor. When we defend against others, we are more accurately defending against the feelings they are prompting in us.

An **addiction** is a repeated pattern of learned behavior that prevents further learning and is a well-entrenched defense against feeling. We habituate to any addiction, meaning we need more to produce the same effect; as addictions escalate, they become self-destructive. Someone who is addicted will often blame the environment for their feeling of helplessness.

Projection is a defense mechanism whereby we make ourselves feel safe by placing what we cannot feel onto others through our speech and actions. We see our issues in the behavior of others but not in ourselves.

A **drama** is an uncanny external play of our disowned feelings in the people around us. The action of the drama contains potential injury and inherent lack of resolution.

Transformation is an internal process of change. In contrast to the drama, transformation requires that we withdraw our feelings from the environment and hold them close. Owning our part often diffuses a drama before it escalates and creates more justification for our original unfelt confusion.

Blind spots will always be there. Even with the best of self-study, we can act from reflexive behaviors that are not paired with what we intend. We know our blind spots by receiving feedback that we have "done it again." This feedback can be difficult to receive but is often pivotal for our growth.

A **shadow** is a large area of dis-owned self. It is often related to the blind spot that is the "tip of the iceberg" of the shadow. Self-reflection is difficult work. Integration is rewarding, but it takes time and patience.

Shame is a challenging feeling to isolate. Shame is some amalgam of the primary emotions of fear, anger and grief that creates a dark, sticky bind suffused with feeling alone, small, impotent, and often stupid. Families and communities have historically used the power of shame to elicit conformity. Shame-dumping is a projection of shame onto others, through words or behavior, to avoid feeling our own burden.

A **complex** is an accumulation of unmet childhood needs that forms an ego identity. Fundamental omission of good care creates a complex compensation pattern, an indirect and unhealthy way of meeting primary needs for support and healthy mirroring. This pattern is called a complex because it has a self-perpetuating and self-fulfilling dysfunction that is unconsciously triggered and highly defended. Most often a complex has a shame core that tightly binds the dysfunctional pattern.

A **personality disorder** is the part of ourselves and our suffering that we cannot see. We become our own suffering. This is distinctly different than anxiety, depression, pain, and physical disease that we can feel and see. Personality disorders are often acted out. The personality disorder is the shadow side, rooted in a complex learned pattern of behavior that sprouts from unmet needs. Two examples are dependency and narcissism. A lack of healthy dependency creates a need that is met through unhealthy dependency. Lack of a healthy mirroring of our feelings and our growing, exploring selves, leads to narcissism. We need others to see us because we cannot see or, more accurately, feel ourselves. The shadow side of teaching yoga is narcissism. Our students will love yoga as we do, and it is important that the praise is for the practices. Gratitude is for our teachers.

Control issues are human and come with the difficulty of managing change and differences. Control issues develop from a healthy need for order that has become rigid rather than negotiable. A need for control of our environment can become a defense against feeling.

Letting go is accepting loss of external control, and the acceptance of our own limits.

An **apology** is a way to relinquish control, and value differences.

Conformity happens when we are less authentic. The more authentic we become the less we need to conform.

The self is free of all complexes; it is an authentic core.

The ego is our agency that can be related with a complex or with the real core. When the ego is aligned with the real self, authenticity blooms.

What you learn about yourself you will revisit many times in many ways. Our impressions and tendencies are deep and need much time, observation, analysis and love to diffuse their hold on us. This is a kind of consolation. We do not have to get it all right. We cannot grow in one leap of insight. Insight puts a wedge in the door of our comprehension, experience will make it wider, meditation will fill the new space with light and air, and gradually the patterns will have little power. To erase them entirely would mean loss of memory. The trace of memory remains. But the ego's relationship with the self becomes the source of guidance, and the confusion that prompts our self-study becomes the gift that spurred our growth.

Ultimately our mental health supports our physical well-being. As we strive to find and keep a healthy balance in our lives, we will naturally confront how we approach life, how we treat others, and we will have to assess our responses and our choices. The purpose of this exercise to dip into areas of ourselves that might remain dim and shapeless. By adding definition, we are empowered to see more clearly and ensure that our progress in holistic.

Listening to others: active listening

We can learn to listen to others in ways that lift both parties beyond individual limits and confusions.

Summarize the statements of others and their concerns. Reflect their language and affirm their experience. Avoid the quick fix.

Ask open questions. Avoid "why;" Use "how" or "what." "Why" suggests that the behavior needs to be defended. "Why are you feeling the way you do?" "What are you feeling?" "How are you feeling?"

Closed questions that have "yes" and "no" answers do not elicit as much information as open questions and they may raise defenses. "Do you feel better?" "Are you taking care of yourself?" are closed questions. "How have you been?" is an open question.

Use simple statements/observations. These statements raise the least defenses. A simple question can imply that something is wrong. "Are you okay?" is a statement that prompts a "yes" or "no" answer and can raise defenses. "Tell me how you are," is an open statement that elicits more information.

Use "I" statements. They establish healthy boundaries. Talking from self raises the opportunity for another to talk freely. "I was wondering how you feel."

ASSIMILATION

Content
➢ Review and learn the eight limbs of yoga in Sanskrit and English.

Contemplation

➢ How do niyamas help us with inabilities or obstacles?

Personal Practice
➢ Practice the niyamas.

➢ What does this mean for you?

Poses

➢ Draw a series that helps you overcome an inability.

Brahmrishi Yoga

The Yogi whose mind is content with knowledge of the self and
of the difference between the self and Nature, who is established in the self,
whose senses are subdued and to whom earth, stone and gold
seem all alike, is integrated.
Bhagavad Gita 6/8

Chapter Eleven – Balance

Samkhya Sutras 16 Ten Objects or Primary Qualities
Complete poses papers
Find internship site

The story of the eleventh chapter: discerning seer from seen, consciousness from energy, self from non-self is the gift of Samkhya. Here we look at our discerning power and how it brings wisdom—all else follows. An introduction to restorative yoga and a survey of pre-natal and post-natal issues both add to our understanding of assisting. Review specific physiological conditions along the lines of exaggeration and depletion.

Contents

We find balance when we accept change.
Devhuti

PHILOSOPHY

Samkhya Sutra 16: Ten Objects or Primary Qualities

The ten root objects are the properties of nature and spirit as they manifest into form. Four belong to both: principal existence, union, disunion and finite existence. Three belong to nature: oneness, purpose, and existing for others. Three belong to spirit: separate from energy, plurality, and non-doer. Discerning the effects of nature and spirit manifesting into form is the analytic practice of Samkhya. This core analysis comes only after we understand that we are mostly lost in this matrix of energy and we need to discern finely and wisely in order to stay clear of the pitfalls of infatuation with the forms of energy.

Analysis underlies yoga and for the serious student, time spent with this analysis bears fruit in a feeling of trust that can only bloom within clear comprehension.

TECHNIQUE

Restorative Yoga

Workshops on restorative yoga are plentiful. Here, a simple summary is: with the use of props and a skilled teacher we gain the obvious physiological benefits of quieting the system, opening the flow of prana, and finding the values of consciousness.

What makes a posture restorative is that the body is fully supported by props, and gravity, not muscular effort, is doing all of the work.

A restorative practice can be beneficial for those recovering from an illness or injury, or during times when we are feeling depleted, physically or psychologically. When approached with a nurturing attitude, these types of postures can help soothe and replenish. When included with other more vigorous work, restorative postures can be particularly helpful in bringing a sense of balance to our experience.

For some who feel a constant pull towards striving and doing, a restorative practice can be a useful challenge for practicing amidst mental distractions. Others, who tend towards tamoguna, should be more cautious.

Pre-natal and Post-natal Issues

Note: Before teaching pre-natal and post-natal yoga, a complete study is needed of the trimesters and contra-indications. The following is only a very brief introduction.

Yoga develops a woman's rapport with her body and a trust in the processes of nature that unfold rapidly during the time of pregnancy. This feeling of comfort with nature translates into the care and comfort of the newborn growing child.

During the pregnancy, the breathing should stay full and steady, without holding. Ujjayi and nadi shodana are useful for balancing and calming.

Pose focus: a sequence of cat/cow, sunbird and child's pose with knees widening as the belly grows. This series helps ease the strain on the supporting ligaments and strengthens and tones abdominal and back muscles essential for holding the increasing weight.

Three trimesters: three varying approaches related with the gunas:

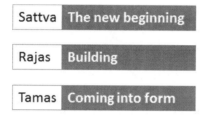

Sattva	The new beginning
Rajas	Building
Tamas	Coming into form

Fourth Trimester: post-natal care

Pre-natal Issues
First trimester: avoid beginning any new form of exercise. If yoga is not a part of the woman's daily routine, then wait for the hardier second trimester. During this first trimester, the future caregiver is adjusting her attitude, developing space for a new primary relationship in her life.

- Changing Ligaments, lengthening and softening.
- Stabilizing poses create a template for the next trimesters.
- Changes in hormones and digestion.
- Need for assimilation and quiet.

Second trimester: begin yoga and work harder in the poses. A time of vigor characterizes this trimester. The baby's heartbeat will commence and with it a direct rapport with the growing child.

- Standing poses, inversions that match the mother's level of yoga.
- Avoid deep twists.

- Initiate habit of avoiding supine and prone positions.
- Develop side-lying habits with blankets for support.
- Careful squatting to help hip ligaments prepare for childbirth.
- Pelvic floor toning.

Third Trimester: less room for the mother to breathe and digest food. The increasing discomfort brings with it the reality of the form of the child and with it, a greater sense of responsibility.

- Gentle movements create more room, helping ease discomfort.
- Increase use of props: wall, chair, blocks, bolsters and blankets.
- Deeper breath awareness and mental focus.
- Reminders about posture, hugging the belly in.
- Work in yoga on a slanted bolster (lying flat on the back should be avoided as the weight of the baby presses on the inferior vena cava and slows return of blood back to the heart, thereby reducing blood flow and oxygen to the baby).

Post-natal Issues
Fourth trimester: time for the baby, mother, father, siblings and other family members to bond. Quiet is important.

- The first post-natal month is a time of less movement so ligaments can shorten and tighten. Allow time for changing hormones.
- Second month brings a need for hip stability, and getting to know the baby.
- Third month, return to yoga with alignment and stability.

Continuing practice with "mommy and me" yoga can help the mother and child bond and play within a gentle, caring environment. The mother's need for independence and exercise will gradually ascend into a time for separate yoga classes.

ASSIMILATION

Content

➢ What are some hyper and hypo conditions of the physiology below?

   – Immune system

   – Blood pressure

   – Thyroid

Contemplation

➢ In restorative poses what are we restoring?

Personal Practice

➢ What is important at the beginning, the middle, and end of your practice?

Poses

➢ Draw 4 series you learned this month that you can add to your teaching.

*Ever applying his mind in this way, the Yogi of controlled mind attains peace
which is the summit of beatitude and which abides in Me.
Bhagavad Gita 6/15*

Chapter Twelve – Sustain

*Samkhya Sutras 17 - 22 Emanation is Accumulation, Fourteen Stages of Being, Threefold
Bondage, Threefold Emancipation, Three proofs, and Freedom
Written research due on Immune System and auto-immune conditions.*

The story of the twelfth chapter: a review of personal experience and wisdom as a guide to practice and teaching. Ethical concerns are reviewed, as is homeostasis with a concluding focus on auto-immune diseases.

Contents

*Every ending is a new beginning
Jin Shin Jyutsu*

PHILOSOPHY

Samkhya Sutra 17: Emanation is Accumulation

Without accumulation of energy into form, we would not see the effects of the projection of energy. The caution of the previous *sutra* is supported and kindly amplified with an additional understanding of nature. Nature will create and accumulate around a developing individual all that is needed for experience and growth. The universe is not merely an accumulation of gross elements; every experience of childhood, livelihood, community and family is the means for us to learn from the results of our previous actions. We have in front of us at all times an accumulation of the perfect means for our growth.

"Emanation is accumulation" is an aphorism that breeds trust in the process of nature unfolding. Life is not random. We are living within a precise system that gives us all we need to move forward with insight, strength, and authenticity. Whatever impressions we carry with us from numerous lives are stored in the *chitta* or *buddhi.* The means for our growth, purification, experience and learning comes through all opportunities and suffering related with family, occupation, children, disease, and accidents that are given to us by nature. The molecules surround the need for the development of the soul. Accumulation is the perfect structure provided by nature in the service of the evolution of consciousness. In other words, *karma* and *klesa* will surround the soul as a means for the continued growth. *Karma,* the results of the intentions of our actions, and *klesa*, the misery that attends misguided action, have the capacity to motivate us to purify our ignorance. Ignorance is the misidentification of self with the forms of energy rather than the infinite field of consciousness.

Samkhya Sutra 18: Fourteen Stages of Evolution of Beings

There are five lower forms of life: vegetable, insect, reptile, bird, and mammal. Human life stands alone as unique. As humans we have developed all instruments and, with the intellect, we have the capacity to realize our self as one with the source of life and to find freedom from suffering. There are eight higher levels of divine life; the soul cannot evolve in the higher levels. We need the experiences that come within a human body to develop divine qualities.

Samkhya Sutra 19: Threefold Bondage

We are bound with attachment and identification to each level of the expression of energy: gross, subtle, causal.

Samkhya Sutra 20: Threefold Emancipation

Liberation comes with detachment from all projections of energy, described as "gradual, disembodied, and singleness."

Samkhya Sutra 21: Three Proofs

Seeing, inference, and testimony. The testimony of others gives us the knowledge we need to move ahead. From that testimony we can infer the truth. Our goal is to see with our own eyes.

Samkhya Sutra 22: Freedom

"If a person comes to realize what I have told, he will be free from the effects of all actions and from bondage. He will never again be the prey of threefold suffering."

The Guest House

This being human is a guest house.
Every morning is a new arrival.

A joy, a depression, a meanness,
some momentary awareness comes
as an unexpected visitor.

Welcome and entertain them all!
Even if they're a crowd of sorrows,
who violently sweep your house
empty of all its furniture,
still, treat each guest honorably.
He may be cleaning you out
for some new delight.

The dark thought, the shame, the malice,
meet them at the door laughing,
and invite them in.

Be grateful for whoever comes
because each has been sent
as a guide from beyond.

Rumi

SUPPLEMENTAL

Ethical Guidelines

As a teacher of Brahmrishi Yoga I agree to ethical standards that respect life. I agree to uphold the dignity and integrity of the tradition of yoga. As a teacher I agree to the life of a student of yoga, and a lifestyle centered on the inward life that sets the standard for outward action. As a teacher, I agree to teach with equanimity, without motive of personal gain.

With my students, in recognition of their trust, I will
 → Respect their personal beliefs and values.
 → Offer my services, regardless of race, creed, color, nation, and/or disabilities of infirmity or age.
 → Avoid actions that conflict with their highest interest
 → Avoid taking unfair advantage, financially, sexually, emotionally, or otherwise.
 → Refrain from a romantic or sexual relationship with a student even if initiated by him/her.

In my professional conduct, I will
 → Offer services I am competent to provide.
 → Not attempt to diagnose a condition, prescribe treatment, or go against medical advice.
 → Make competent referrals, as needed.
 → Continue to study in order to serve.
 → Uphold the integrity of yoga by behaving in a professional manner with regard to other teachers.
 → Be fair in my business dealings.
 → Deal lawfully in all business and accounting transactions.

In advertising, I will
 → Make no false claims as to the benefit of yoga or my classes.
 → Represent my training and qualifications, abilities and affiliations, unambiguously and accurately.
 → Not falsely accept the endorsement, representation, or sponsorship of any organization.

I understand that any report of my breach of this code will be investigated and that I am at risk for losing my certification with Brahmrishi Yoga Teacher Training.

_____

Print name

_____

Signature   *Date*

248

Sample Health Form

Brahmrishi Yoga

Woman's Resource Center, Kent State University
Registration and Release

Name _____ Age _____ Phone _____
Email _____
Address _____

Yoga history:
- — Previous experience with yoga

- — Regular practice, studio or home, and frequency

- — Other forms of exercise and frequency

- — Physical limitations

Medical history:
- — Accidents, surgeries (dates if recent), medications

Expectations of these sessions:

Background:
- — Occupation

- — Specific life challenges

Yoga is an integrative movement and breathing practice. I understand the intention of the instructor and the facility is to inform, educate, guide and assist in my health and well-being.

I understand that I am solely responsible for my health, safety and well-being. I agree to inform the teacher of any movement I cannot safely perform and will avoid movement that may be injurious. I hereby waive any and all claims against the instructor arising out of my actions during the instructions of such yoga practice.

Signed: _____ Date:_____

ASSIMILATION

Content

➤ From your review of physiology, describe the significance of the field of study called Psychoneuroimmunoendocrinology (PNIE).

Contemplation

➤ Is there an area of ethics that feels ambiguous?

➤ How do we address exaggeration and depletion in practice?

Personal Practice

➤ What makes a practice sustainable?

Poses

➤ Draw a key pose for immune balance.

Appendix

Internship

For this therapeutic yoga training the series of poses you will teach during your final practicum hour and internship will be based on the needs of your body. Within the vinyasa track, you are responsible for instructing a vinyasa series. You will present this series to your training group in the latter half of the course for support and feedback. What works for you will be your starting point for teaching others. While teaching others, your observation of their needs is a continuing focus for your learning. You are required to teach a series of six sessions, a minimum of sixty minutes each. Two of the sessions will be observed by a practicum teacher who will give you specific feedback.

Written work

Writing is a way of learning the material and formulating your own thoughts. Teaching yoga well requires that we gain skill in absorbing knowledge and in articulating clearly.

There are three main papers:

One on the "Value of Yoga"

This topic is purposefully general so that you can express what is most personal and interesting to you. This can be a story-line or it can be based in research. Minimum two pages.

Two separate papers on a series of poses:

These papers are the most challenging of all written assignments. Start soon. Each paper includes a sequence of four poses that suits your body and that you wish to teach. Why anatomy? Simple and powerful instructions are based in a comprehension of anatomy. Each paper includes:

- Stick figures of the poses and instructions for creating the asanas.
- Annamayakosha:
  - What is vital muscular action?—keep it simple.
  - What is lengthened?
  - How does this pose *prepare for* or *release into* the next pose?
  - Be specific about the muscles and aware of basic agonist/antagonist pairs.
- Pranamayakosha: What "opens" and makes the pose "feel good?"
- Manomayakosha: How does this affect the mind?

Assignments

These written assignments are to include a definition of terms and then your personal reflection or research. There is no need to make these lengthy.

Below is a timeline. Internship requirement is included.

Chapter Three – Three Gunas

Begin assignment on the Three Gunas & Teaching Styles, related with your personal doshas. How does who you are impact how you might teach?

Chapter Four – Observer and observed

Written assignment due on the Three Gunas & Teaching Styles.

Chapter Five – Suffering

Begin written assignment on the Klesas. There are five ways we make ourselves suffer. Define and offer your personal reflection on where you see yourself within these terms.

Begin Poses papers: Choose an outline of the sequences.
Choose a topic for the Value of Yoga paper.

Chapter Six – Practice

Written assignment due on the Klesas.
Begin research assignment on the Nervous System, the Brain, Yoga, and Meditation. Use internet research or any reading material you have found. Useful: www.dana.org

Continue Poses papers: Adding to Annamayakosha.
Plan your internship setting and time.

Chapter Seven – Breathing

Revisit Poses papers: adding more elements of breathing.
Continue with the Value of Yoga Paper.

Chapter Eight – Restraint

Begin assignment on Yamas and Niyamas. Choose one of each vow and observance and contemplate your relationship with them.
Written assignment due on the Nervous System, the Brain, Yoga and Meditation.

Chapter Nine – Space and Wind

Written assignment due on Yamas and Niyamas.
Written paper due on the Value of Yoga.

Chapter Ten – Meditation

Begin written assignment researching an aspect of the Immune System, particularly within auto-immune conditions.

Chapter Eleven – Balance

Complete Poses papers.
Find Internship site.

Chapter Twelve – Sustain

Written assignment due on Immune System and auto-immune conditions.

61072446R00146

Made in the USA
Charleston, SC
12 September 2016